the Heck
Do I Do
with My
Life?

Praise for the book

Ravi has always offered thoughtful frameworks for solving complicated problems. As the world grows in complexity, Ravi's guidance to be curious and adaptable has never been more relevant.

—**Bill Gates**

The digital revolution that is transforming business and society has created both extraordinary challenges and unprecedented opportunities. In his insightful and compelling book, Ravi Venkatesan offers practical perspectives on the mindset, skills and strategies that lead to impact and happiness.

—**Satya Nadella**, Chairman and CEO, Microsoft Corporation

Ravi has taken a lifetime of learning and condensed it into a deeply personal account of what it takes to flourish in this period of extreme change. *What the Heck Do I Do with My Life?* is full of pragmatic advice as well as wisdom, on meaningful living. It should inspire, challenge and most of all, help you find your purpose!

—**Nandan Nilekani,** Chairman and Co-founder, Infosys and Founding Chairman, Unique Identification Authority of India (UIDAI)

Flourishing in our VUCA world requires intentional choices that will bring sense and sensibility to our lives. Ravi's book is an invaluable and must-read guide for this.

—**Kiran Mazumdar-Shaw**, Founder and Executive Chairperson, Biocon Limited

In this deeply thought-provoking book, Ravi simultaneously contemplates big philosophical questions while delivering common sense advice on how to design a successful and satisfying life in a century of profound change and stunning possibilities. It is filled with inspiring stories and insights. I highly recommend it.

—**P. V. Sindhu,** Two-time Olympic medallist and Badminton World Champion

What the Heck the Heck Do I Do with My Life?

How to Flourish in
Our Turbulent Times

RAVI VENKATESAN

RUPA

Published by
Rupa Publications India Pvt. Ltd 2022
7/16, Ansari Road, Daryaganj
New Delhi 110002

Sales centres:
Allahabad Bengaluru Chennai
Hyderabad Jaipur Kathmandu
Kolkata Mumbai

ISBN: 978-93-5520-290-1

Seventh impression 2022

10 9 8 7

The moral right of the author has been asserted.

Printed at Thomson Press India Ltd., Faridabad

'…a person's true potential is unknown (and unknowable); …it's impossible to foresee what can be accomplished with years of passion, toil and training.'[*]

—Carol S. Dweck

[*]Carol S. Dweck, *Mindset: The New Psychology of Success*, Random House, 2006.

Contents

Preface

I started work on this book-project nearly 10 years ago, but this is a very different book from the one I set out to write. During the decade, the world changed significantly and my understanding of the world has changed even more. As a result, this book too has turned out differently.

My motivation to write this book came from a growing number of requests for career and life advice from people. It began with the talks I used to give at employee gatherings at Microsoft India, starting around 2005. I would talk about our business, but would invariably end with some introspection and personal learning. People quickly forgot what I said about business but remembered and appreciated my homilies on careers, success and happiness. So, many 'Microsofties' started coming to me for some mentoring and advice. I enjoyed this part of my job a lot.

In 2011, I wrapped up my innings at Microsoft and stepped off the beaten path. I didn't have much clarity about what I wanted to do next but was determined to be a free agent, never again an employee. I experimented my way into the future— a process that was ultimately rewarding but most uncomfortable in the beginning. I first wrote about this journey in 2013 as a series of articles in *The Economic Times*, titled 'Crossing the

Mid-Career Chasm'.[1] The ideas and my candour resonated with over a million readers, many of whom wrote in hoping for more personalized advice. Fortunately, this was the time when LinkedIn was emerging as a platform for professionals, and I began posting short reflections on leadership, adapting to change and so on. One post in particular, 'India's IT Party Is Over. Reinvent Yourself or Suffer',[2] struck a chord with a lot of readers and got an astonishing two million views and many comments. I realized that there was something big happening. As the pace of change in the world accelerated, more and more people were confused, disoriented, anxious, overwhelmed and depressed, searching for answers. Reading through all the comments that poured in, I sensed that a fundamental question for many of us is: 'How can I be successful and happy in this turbulent world? What should I do with my life?'

The question, 'What do I do with my life?' is a recurring theme that seems to pop up across life stages. Young people today are confronted with fewer jobs, a bewildering array of choices and a crumbling planet. Their education, designed for a stable world that no longer exists, leaves them unprepared, lacking the mindset and skills needed to succeed in a fast-changing world. What should I study? Where are the best jobs going to be in the future? What skills should I try to acquire? What jobs are least likely to be automated? Should I even bother

---

[1]Ravi Venkatesan, 'Crossing the Mid-Career Chasm', *The Economic Times*, 26 April 2013, https://economictimes.indiatimes.com/blogs/Musings/crossing-the-mid-career-chasm/. Accessed on 19 October 2021.
[2]Ravi Venkatesan, 'India's IT Party Is Over. Reinvent Yourself or Suffer', LinkedIn, 31 May 2015, https://www.linkedin.com/pulse/indias-party-over-reinvent-yourself-suffer-ravi-venkatesan. Accessed on 19 October 2021.

with a job or focus on starting something on my own or be self-employed? These are often asked questions. The people they most turn to for guidance—parents, teachers and elders—can only share what worked for them, but the context has changed so much that their advice is often wrong; for instance, they would say 'Don't take risks', 'Aim for a government job' or 'Study coding because that is where the jobs are'.

People in their 30s and 40s face different challenges. Usually, their life is not what they expected it to turn out as. Life and others seem to be passing by them. There are insecurities, the fear of missing out (FOMO) and a desire to make it big before growing old. Many are trapped in jobs and situations they don't enjoy, often working for people they don't quite respect, but not knowing what changes to make. There are thousands of advice peddlers serving this segment; a quick search on Amazon for books on career success yields 10,000 results with strategies for success in life and at work. There is also an ocean of content on related topics on YouTube and LinkedIn. Clearly, there is an insatiable desire for advice on what to do with your life and how to be successful and, equally, a ready supply of advice and opinions, but it is a real challenge to separate the wheat from the chaff.

Finally, there are a growing number of people who, like me, are in their 50s or older. On the one hand, we are living longer, have a desire to remain productive till much later and need to earn some money, only a few have pensions or any meaningful social security net. On the other, the world has a great preference for younger people with the newest skills and great energy. The reality is that once you cross 50, you are living on borrowed time, with the risk of being displaced by a software or, more likely, by a younger version of you. So, what can I do to stay relevant and useful? This is also a time when many people feel a higher calling and realize that there are other dimensions to life, especially the spiritual. The desire to give back, to be in service of something greater than oneself grows louder. But where and how do you start? So, we are back once again to the recurring question, 'What do I do with my life?'

The way my generation and my parents' generation approached the challenge of composing one's life was to emulate people who we considered successful. It was a simpler world in which there were far fewer pathways to success; there was also far less focus on being exceptional. Being a decent person, raising a good family and living a contented life defined success for most people around me. The key was to become clear fairly early on about your role models and success archetype (scientist, engineer, doctor, civil servant, writer, etc.), understand the choices they made and start working diligently. This may mean studying engineering or medicine regardless of your interest or aptitude because that is where most jobs were. This approach worked well for me; I locked in on a model of success quite early on and then maintained a laser focus on getting there. (It is a different matter that when I got there, the goalposts had moved, which I write about in the last chapter.)

Much of the 'advice industry' still operates in this mode. Success gurus either reflect on what worked for them or try to extract the recipes of apparently successful people's lives. When done well, this can be inspiring and useful, as Steve Jobs was in his commencement speech at Stanford University. It can be misleading, and even dangerous, in a social media-fuelled world, where everyone has an opinion and there is no dearth of self-proclaimed experts and charlatans peddling advice.

The core problem is that the world is a lot more complicated today and changing incredibly fast, so what worked well in the past may not be so relevant now. Also, what worked for you may not work for me. In the inimitable words of baseball star Yogi Berra, 'The future ain't what it used to be.' The defining feature of this century is likely to be the magnitude and rate of change which is unprecedented in human history. The world is becoming more fluid and the phrase 'volatile, uncertain, complex and ambiguous' (VUCA) is frequently used to describe it. There are clear signs everywhere that we need new ways to think about our world and our place in it. Our old ideas about work, success, lifestyle, etc., no longer work. They have not worked for a long time but it took a pandemic to help us see this.

So, what we need is a paradigm shift—a whole new way of looking at these things. Following advice from the old paradigm may not be so helpful. What advice do you give people on what skills will be useful when jobs of the future are still being invented? Will 'jobs' even exist or are we moving to a world of projects and gig work? Success, for many people, used to mean having a stable job, a good salary and climbing some ladder in terms of title, responsibility and influence. Today, there are so many different career pathways, so many ways to make a life and a living. Success can mean many more things and can take many more forms. So, my aim in this book is to shy away from success strategies and try to get you to explore deeper and more fundamental drivers of life.

Think of an iceberg; while 90 per cent of it lies below

the water, only about 10 per cent is visible above the water. This is a good metaphor for success and satisfaction in life. You can think of what is visible above the water as the strategies, tactics and skills that will help you be more successful in your career. This is the level at which many success advisors operate.

However, what lies below the surface is much more significant. What lies beneath are our mostly implicit assumptions about fundamental things such as:

- Identity—'Who am I?', 'Who am I if I am not a "manager in company X"?'
- Purpose—'Why am I here?', 'How will I measure my life when I look back at it?'
- Mindset—the stories and assumptions we have about everything including ourselves and others, how the world operates and how we define success and failure

Our beliefs about these things have a greater influence on who we are, the choices we make, what we accomplish and how satisfied we are with life, and so I focus on these aspects.

The central thesis of my book is this: the only way to deal with a fast-changing VUCA world is to live intentionally and be anchored in your beliefs, purpose, commitments and core relationships. But for that, you need to know what these are, which means you have to become more intentional about your life. It is simply too risky to drift through life. Also, while it may feel as though the world is unforgiving and teeming with formidable challenges, it is important to remember that it is equally filled with extraordinary opportunities. So, this is overwhelmingly a time to be optimistic and not be consumed by anxiety and pessimism. There are more opportunities than ever before in history; if you are adventurous, positive and have the right mindset and skills, the chances are that you will flourish. If you sit around wondering why the world is collapsing and wait to be rescued, life will likely be tough and unforgiving.

As you go through the chapters in this book, there is a risk that some of you might think, 'Well, that's easy for Ravi to say from his privileged perch, but my reality could not be more different,' and discount or dismiss some important idea. That is why I began this book with American psychologist Carol Dweck's statement that the true potential of any person is unknown and unknowable. With a combination of intentionality, years of toil and reasonable luck, most of us can accomplish more than we might imagine possible. My own story is that of an ordinary person who had extraordinary experiences and I think this is possible for most (though not all) of us. I have tried as much as possible to share my doubts and struggles to help make the point that 'success' is subjective, hard-won and does not necessarily lead to contentment and happiness.

As you read, you will also find yourself disagreeing with many of my ideas and assertions. That is perfectly fine. What matters is that you think hard about each idea, come to your conclusions and implement a few things that you find useful. Think of the ideas here as Lego blocks; examine them, see what fits and feel free to discard the rest. My primary objective is to provoke and challenge you and get you to intentionally design your life rather than just drift through it.

Good luck!

Adapt ~~or Perish~~ and Flourish

'A snake that cannot shed its skin must die!'
—Friedrich Nietzsche

∽

I often get asked for career advice or invited to give a talk on how to be successful. There is an underlying presumption that having been reasonably successful, I will share insights or recipes for success that might be useful to my audience. It is, of course, flattering to be asked, but I invariably begin with a cautionary disclaimer that much of my professional life and success was in a context that has changed profoundly. What worked for me and my generation may not be that relevant today.

For much of the past century, the passport out of poverty to the middle class and then, to affluence, was a good education, particularly, higher education. You got into a good school, worked really hard to get into an even better college or university, landed a job with a good organization and then worked hard to climb the ladder as far as possible, taking care to not upset your bosses. If you were academically sorted, you became a scientist, engineer, doctor or perhaps a chartered accountant (CA). In my parents' generation, a good career involved getting a job with the government and then entering a tunnel from which you emerged with a satisfying retirement, 40 years later. My generation found better prospects in private-sector jobs; many of us escaped to the United States (US) or some other country in search of better opportunities than what pre-liberalization India offered. We had it particularly good because we had not one, but two massive tides that lifted millions of people to a better life. The first tide was globalization—the integration of China and then India into the global system—which created incredible opportunities. Then came the Internet and, with it, the technology industry, which is today a $5-trillion economy. This created extraordinary opportunities for anyone with reasonable education and drive. A lot of success is just about the good luck of being in the right place at the right time with the right attitude.

The situation today is completely different. We are confronted with a set of conditions called VUCA. I will talk about this more later but, essentially, multiple forces combine to create a future that is impossible to predict. We will face a lot of turbulence, extreme events and rapid change. This creates a very difficult environment for all of us—for individuals, companies, institutions and countries. Those who can adapt and navigate the turbulence will do well, while those who cannot, suffer greatly. As Warren Buffett famously said after the financial crisis of 2008, 'A rising tide lifts all boats but only when the tide goes out do you discover who's been swimming naked.' So, the key to success in the twenty-first century is the ability to adapt to and thrive on complexity, uncertainty and change.

Virtually everyone knows how dinosaurs became extinct. About 66 million years ago, a massive rock, the size of Manhattan, slammed into the earth, near Mexico. The collision had the energy of a billion atomic bombs and sent 25 trillion tons of debris into the atmosphere. The dust and soot from the impact prevented any sunlight from reaching the planet's surface for months, killing most of the plant life, extinguishing the phytoplankton in the oceans and causing the amount of oxygen in the atmosphere to plummet. After the fires died down, Earth plunged into a deep freeze and food chains, both in the sea and on land, collapsed. More than 99.99 per cent of all living organisms on Earth died. About 75 per cent of all species went extinct, including dinosaurs.

Not everyone is aware that this catastrophe directly led to the rise of mammals and, in turn, us. Amongst the survivors of the holocaust were a few small early mammals that demonstrated incredible adaptability to the new conditions. In just 10 million years, the number and diversity of mammals exploded. This period saw the rise of the first whales, bats and rodents. Over the next several million years, mammals evolved rapidly, adapting to new habitats and food resources, including flowering plants and insects. New kinds of forests appeared, offering habitats for tree-dwelling mammals; the first primates appeared about 50 million years ago, and eventually, some 45 million years later, humans.

Are you wondering what this story has to do with you? Well, everything. Adaptation to extreme change is the fundamental challenge of the twenty-first century.

Evolutionary biologists and palaeontologists use the term 'punctuated equilibrium', which means that in the history of the earth, there are often long, quiet periods when everything is fairly stable and evolution happens incrementally. These stable periods are punctuated by bursts of sudden and dramatic change, triggered by an event, such as the asteroid strike.

These periods of sudden change pose a huge adaptive challenge. Several species, such as the dinosaurs, struggle to adapt quickly and thus become extinct. Conversely, those species, such as the early mammals, which can adapt and thrive become the new dominant species. This observation led Charles Darwin to note that in nature, it is not the strongest of species that survives nor the most intelligent, but rather the ones that are the most responsive to change. COVID-19 offers a graphic example of punctuated equilibrium and adaptation. The pandemic has been an enormous shock to the whole world, but it impacted the weak, unhealthy, marginalized and vulnerable the most. Some individuals, companies, states and countries have been able to adapt to the shock much better than others. Several firms have closed down, millions of people have lost employment and income. Overall, it has resulted in dramatically greater inequality both across and within countries.

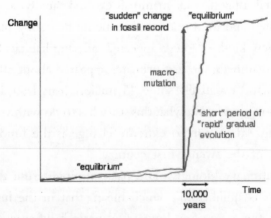

Source: Diagram of alternative explanations of punctuated equilibrium, Wikimedia Commons/Ian Alexander

It is a good, if brutal, lesson on shocks and adaptation, and there will be many more shocks in the period of extreme change that we are going through, after many decades of relative stability. The story of the twenty-first century is fundamentally going to be about how we adapted to extreme change as our world is set to change more this century than in all of human history. How well are you likely to adapt? Are you likely to be a mammal or a dinosaur?

What is driving this much change? In his terrific book *Ten Years to Midnight*, my friend Blair Sheppard, who leads strategy and leadership at PricewaterhouseCoopers (PwC), describes how a number of powerful forces are colliding to create a perfect storm for us.[1] In a nice play on words, he calls these forces 'ADAPT' (Asymmetry, Disruption, Age, Polarization and Trust).

Asymmetry: Asymmetry is the accelerating disparity in wealth among individuals, among countries and among regions within countries, and between generations. The statistics are staggering. In India, 73 per cent of the new wealth generated in 2017 went to the top one per cent of the population.[2] One businessman, Gautam Adani, added $35.2 billion to his wealth in 2021 despite India's economy shrinking by 10 per cent as

---

[1]Blair H. Sheppard, *Ten Years to Midnight: Four Urgent Global Crises and Their Strategic Solutions*, Berrett-Koehler Publishers, 2020. A perfect storm is an event in which a rare combination of circumstances drastically aggravates the event. The term is used as an analogy for an unusually severe storm that results from a rare combination of meteorological phenomena.

[2]The Wire Staff, 'Richest 1% Cornered 73% of Wealth Generated in India in 2017: Oxfam Survey', *The Wire,* 22 January 2018, https://thewire.in/economy/richest-1-cornered-73-wealth-generated-india-2017-oxfam-survey. Accessed on 1 December 2021.

a result of COVID-19. Of course, this was eclipsed by the
$70 billion that Jeff Bezos added to his fortunes even as 40
million Americans filed for unemployment post COVID-19.
Collectively, American billionaires saw their personal wealth
increase by $1 trillion in 2020. COVID-19 exacerbated the
divide between countries and also within countries; smaller,
informal firms struggled to survive even as Big Tech firms
like Apple and Amazon flourished. The majority of people are
getting left behind and are resentful and angry and distrust
the existing system and institutions which have created such
disparity. This spells a bit of trouble for many societies and
the whole world too.

Disruption: Technology and climate change are powerful and
interlinked disruptive forces. The Fourth Industrial Revolution
will deliver mind-boggling breakthroughs and innovations but is
raising enormous challenges such as the dominance of Big Tech
giants such as Amazon and Google, the undermining of society
and democracy by social media companies like Facebook, the
impact of artificial intelligence (AI) and robotics on jobs, and
the risks posed to humanity by the rise of the machines.

Climate is the most important disruption facing humanity
but the catastrophic impact of humans on the planet extends
beyond climate; it includes the destruction of irreplaceable
habitats, mass extinction of species and the occurrence of
pandemics like COVID-19, to name a few. We have only
seen the tip of the iceberg of all this so far, the worst is yet
to come. And, of course, it is the poorest and weakest who
will again suffer the most.

Age: Age or demographics will pose new challenges. Regions with young populations, such as South Asia and Africa, will have the growing challenge of creating jobs and economic opportunities. In India, for instance, one million young people turn 18 every month and start looking for work; but for over a decade, employment growth has been half of the population growth and so, unemployment was at a historic high even pre-COVID. It is much the same story across Africa. AI and cheap robots will make the challenge even greater. Wealthy countries have a different problem with ageing populations adding pressure to social security and health systems. More and more people will run out of savings and investments and be unable to retire; they will need a safety net, which will strain public finance even more.

Polarization: The world has been fracturing along various divisions—religion, race, education, income and ideas, as people's faith in leaders and institutions has started breaking down. These divisions have been stoked and amplified by opportunists everywhere. The last presidential elections in the US showed just how polarized America has become; one editorial summed it up stating, 'Let us face the bitter truth. We are two countries and neither of them is going to disappear or be conquered anytime soon.'[3] The same can be said for many countries, including India, which is rapidly becoming a nation of differences rather than of diversity. Polarization, with its evil twin distrust, destroys our ability to work together to solve problems and make progress.

---

[3]George Packer, 'Face the Bitter Truth', *The Atlantic*, 5 November 2020, https://www.theatlantic.com/ideas/archive/2020/11/theres-no-escaping-who-we-have-become/616992/. Accessed on 19 October 2021.

Trust: All around the world, trust in government, business and institutions is declining dramatically. Why does trust matter? When people don't trust leaders or institutions, they resist. You could see this in the response to COVID-19 as people in many parts of the world refused to wear masks and follow social distancing guidelines or challenged the safety of vaccines. You can also see this in the massive farmer and citizen protests in India opposing the reform of agricultural laws that were intended to help farmers.

Research from Harvard shows that countries with low levels of trust invariably find themselves in a downward spiral, a 'distrust trap' of greater regulation and lower economic growth.[4] Such societies are unable to come together and solve problems for the greater good. In these countries, people are more likely to shape public policy and do business in ways that benefit their own family, social class, tribe and religion. They are likely to support policies that redistribute wealth in their favour rather than policies that grow the overall economic pie. People are more likely to bribe officials, steal and engage in fraud.

The five forces called ADAPT are like the 'five' horsemen of the Apocalypse; they are each powerful and transformative but the interaction between them can magnify their impact. For instance, the joblessness resulting from more automation is amplified by the increase in life expectancy which results in even more people wanting or needing to be productive and employed. So, these forces can create a perfect storm and a massive adaptation challenge for each one of us.

---

[4]Philippe Aghion, Yann Algan, Pierre Cahuc and Andrei Shleifer, 'Regulation and Distrust', *The Quarterly Journal of Economics*, Volume 125, Issue 3, August 2010.

What could so much change mean for you? Let us take a look at just three of the many possible ways they can impact you.

1. How will the changing nature of work affect you professionally?
2. What are the implications of living till you're nearly 100?
3. And finally, a surprising question, 'Could chaos engulf the place where you live?'

Question 1: How will the changing nature of work affect you professionally?

The rapidly changing nature of work has made debates on 'the future of work' a red-hot topic. Scarcely a week goes by without a new report on this issue by some consulting company, think tank or organization like the World Economic Forum. Here are three predictions that I believe in.

i.   Technology will not only destroy many jobs while creating new ones, but will also change every single job:
Even before the pandemic, the world of work—of jobs, employment and entrepreneurship—was being disrupted by technology, especially AI. It has been observed that we always overestimate the change that will occur in the next two years and underestimate the change that will occur in the next 10. This seems particularly true of AI which is a real tsunami. The reality is that intelligent machines are catching up with and surpassing human capability at specific tasks at a stunning rate. Here are some examples:

Software is getting better than most humans at programming.

An unsupervised machine translation model trained on GitHub projects can translate 90 per cent of functions from C++ into Java and Python functions into C++ and successfully pass all tests.

Given a broken programme and diagnostic feedback (compiler error messages), an AI programme called Dr Repair finds the erroneous line of code and generates a repaired line.

Google's AutoML is at a point where it can create machine learning software that is more efficient than what most developers can create. AI is at the tipping point where it has surpassed most humans in the creation of AI.

Now think about the common advice that everyone should learn basic coding and the rise of coding schools and programmes everywhere. Is someone with basic programming skills likely to find a job five years from now? Think about the implications of this for the hundreds of thousands of software developers and testers all over the world, particularly in India.

In medicine, algorithms for medical diagnosis are now able to perform at the level of the top 25 per cent of all doctors, putting them in the category of expert clinicians. AI-based systems can outperform human radiologists in reliably detecting cancer. They are also improving very rapidly unlike their human counterparts.

The start-up LawGeex ran tests to compare the effectiveness of lawyers with that of an AI platform in assessing the quality of non-disclosure agreements (NDAs). The study involved 20 lawyers with dozens of years of experience in top companies such as Goldman Sachs and Cisco as well as LawGeex's proprietary AI platform. Participants evaluated the risks contained in five different NDA agreements by searching for 30 specific legal points. LawGeex's AI showed an average accuracy rate of 94 per cent, whereas the lawyers achieved an average of 85 per cent. The highest-performing lawyer in the study achieved 94 per cent accuracy, thus matching the AI. On an average, they required 92 minutes to accomplish the task, while the AI analysed all the documents in 26 seconds.[5]

I could go on and on, but you get the picture. AI has closed in on and often exceeded human capability at narrow tasks astonishingly fast. And as each advance builds on other advances, the capability of AI will get exponentially better. We haven't seen anything yet.

This will have enormous consequences for productivity and jobs. In some cases, AI will enhance human capability and be a tool or assistant. But in other cases, it will replace humans. I believe that a quarter of all jobs, particularly those involving repetitive tasks, like those of cashiers or hazardous ones handled by warehouse or manufacturing workers, are likely to be rapidly automated. Another third of jobs are at medium risk, as a machine could do between 30–70 per cent of their tasks. This includes accountants, lawyers, stockbrokers, programmers and radiologists. Some 40 per cent of jobs are at low risk.

[5]PRNewswire, 'Artificial Intelligence More Accurate Than Lawyers for Reviewing Contracts, New Study Reveals', 26 February 2018, *Cision PRNewswire*, https://www.prnewswire.com/news-releases/artificial-intelligence-more-accurate-than-lawyers-for-reviewing-contracts-new-study-reveals-300603781.html. Accessed on 2 December 2021.

These are particularly those that involve feelings or emotional intelligence, such as nursing, entertainment or situations with high variability such as teaching and law enforcement. Like a rising tide that covers more and more rocks, AI will engulf more roles and jobs as its capability improves, which it will, exponentially.[6]

While AI and automation may destroy many jobs over the next decade, over a longer horizon—10 years and beyond— the impact of technology on jobs is likely to be much more positive. We are in the early stages of what is called 'The Fourth Industrial Revolution', which is a way of describing technological advances in multiple fields that are blurring the boundaries between the physical, digital and biological worlds. It refers to a fusion of advances in computing, AI, the Internet of Things (IoT), materials, molecular biology, genetics and many other fields that are coming together to create completely new possibilities. Possibilities such as engineering viruses to create batteries with no toxic waste, yielding the breakthrough to limitless zero-carbon energy; using a common protein to purify drinking water; employing IoT and machine learning

---

[6]'The Impact of Artificial Intelligence on Work', Royal Society, https://royalsociety.org/-/media/policy/projects/ai-and-work/evidence-synthesis-the-impact-of-AI-on-work.PDF?la=en-GB&hash=A7BBFC34940375F2EE5548A1320F1F72. Accessed on 19 September 2021.

Mark Muro, Robert Maxim and Jacob Whiton, 'Automation and Artificial Intelligence: How machines are affecting people and places', Brookings Institute, https://www.brookings.edu/research/automation-and-artificial-intelligence-how-machines-affect-people-and-places/. Accessed on 19 September 2021.

Carl Benedikt Frey, *The Technology Trap: Capital, Labor, and Power in the Age of Automation*, Princeton University Press, 2019.

Daniel Susskind, *A World Without Work: Technology, Automation, and How We Should Respond*, Metropolitan Books, 2020.

to dramatically improve crop yields and driverless electric cars and intelligent robots that can interact seamlessly with humans.

The Fourth Industrial Revolution is transforming the way we live and work and will create immense entrepreneurial opportunities, and many new types of jobs that we cannot even imagine. Even a decade ago, roles such as data scientist, social media manager, content moderator, cloud architect and drone operator did not exist. This means that it is fairly pointless asking questions such as, 'What do you want to be/do when you grow up?' or try to learn skills for jobs that seem to be hot right now. Hot jobs are a moving target and what matters is the ability to continuously adapt to changing scenarios, learn new skills and move to where the new opportunities are.

The prospects for jobs get better as we see a crisis as the source of opportunity. Climate change is emerging as the existential crisis of humanity and solving it will drive a tsunami of entrepreneurial opportunity that will dwarf the Internet economy. Many experts estimate that decarbonizing the world and learning to live more sustainably is likely to create a new $50-trillion economy that is 10 times greater than the Internet economy and 20 times the gross domestic product (GDP) of India. It is not just about solar panels and electric vehicles. We need to rethink where and how we live, reinvent green steel and green cement, devise new heating and cooling systems and rethink how we grow and distribute food. Millions of people will need to migrate and be resettled. All of these challenges present enormous opportunities for inventors, entrepreneurs and investors. Think about the number of unicorns, the new billionaires, the number of firms and new jobs that such a massive overhaul of systems will create over the coming decades.

For those who are entrepreneurial-minded, willing to move to the biggest challenges and learn new things, the perfect storm is also the opportunity of a lifetime.

ii.   The idea of a job itself is becoming obsolete:
The idea of a job, that is, a stable contract between an employee and a company where, in exchange for the former's time and talent, the latter gives a decent wage, healthcare and other benefits alongside opportunities to learn and grow, is obsolete. It is an artefact of the industrial age that is fast disappearing.

There are multiple reasons for this. Companies are being forced to transform or perish. Even once-iconic firms, such as GE, IBM and Boeing, are being humbled, disrupted and forced to lay off large numbers of people. COVID-19 has accelerated automation, restructuring, closures and layoffs. There is no such thing as a stable or secure job anymore (except perhaps in government which stubbornly remains unaccountable in most countries). As employers themselves are subject to upheavals and uncertainty, they are becoming more short term and transactional, using more flexible labour arrangements—more outsourcing, more subcontractors and gig workers. So, the core of long-term employees is shrinking rapidly. There are subtrends as well, such as a preference for younger workers who have more contemporary skills, more drive and can be paid less. So too is the continuous, culling process under the guise of performance management. Even chief executive officers (CEOs) are not safe; the median tenure of a CEO in the US is 5.5 years and declining.

Remote working or work from home (WfH) is another trend that has accelerated due to COVID-19. Remote and hybrid work are here to stay. That is because many of us prefer working at least partially from home; it results in higher productivity, better health and satisfaction. Employers like the benefits of lower infrastructure costs, greater productivity and, most of all, the ability to access talent anywhere. As a result, the use of gig-workers, consultants and contracts is likely to accelerate.

So, you can see why we need to rethink our ideas around stable employment, jobs and careers; they are artefacts of a world that is fast disappearing. The writer Charles Handy predicts that there will be broadly three categories of workers in the future.[7] First is the category of 'creatives', which includes software architects, artists, entertainers and content creators. The second group, forming the vast majority, he calls 'caregivers', which includes frontline workers who perform essential services such as nursing, package delivery and sanitation workers. Finally, there are 'custodians'. Organizations will not disappear and you will still need a few people to manage work, processes and infrastructure but there will be fewer such managers. A fast-growing number of workers will be self-employed, with various kinds of flexible contractual arrangements. It is a different world.

iii. Brace yourself for greater inequality:
Inequality will widen as the job market becomes increasingly segregated into low-skill/low-pay and high-skill/high-pay roles. A Korn Ferry report estimates that companies can expect to add $2.5 trillion to their annual cost of labour by 2030 as a result of a global shortage of highly skilled workers that

---

[7]Charles Handy, *21 Letters on Life and Its Challenges* (Kindle Edition), Cornerstone Digital (2019).

could dramatically drive up salaries for the most in-demand talent.[8] In contrast to the lucky few who live in the right zip codes and have the requisite hot skills, most people will be stuck in subsistence-level jobs with no security, few benefits and no opportunity for advancement. An important report of the future of work shows data that once again, COVID-19 trends have accelerated job growth in high-skill/high-wage roles and further disrupted low-skill/low-wage jobs.[9] This will force many more workers to switch occupations as demand for data-entry operators, retail workers or low-end office support jobs declines.

Even a higher education degree may not help. For much of the last century, higher education was viewed as a passport to greater prosperity and success. Lately though, the correlation seems to have broken down as the rate of job creation has slowed. In pre-COVID India, 35 per cent of the youth who possessed a graduate or post-graduate degree were unemployed; a young person with a higher-education degree is, shockingly, five times as likely to be unemployed as her illiterate counterpart.[10] The numbers are far worse post-COVID. This reflects as much on the quality of the jobs being created—low-wage/repetitive work—which are not aspirational as it is a commentary on

[8]'The Salary Surge', Korn Ferry, https://www.kornferry.com/insights/this-week-in-leadership/the-salary-surge. Accessed on 19 September 2021.

[9]'The future of work after COVID-19', 18 February 2021, McKinsey Global Institute, https://www.mckinsey.com/featured-insights/future-of-work/the-future-of-work-after-covid-19. Accessed on 22 November 2021.

[10]Shamika Ravi, 'View: Here's What We Know for Sure about Jobs in India', *The Economic Times*, 18 April 2019, https://economictimes.indiatimes.com/news/economy/policy/heres-what-we-know-for-sure-about-jobs-in-india/articleshow/68916626.cms. Accessed on 19 September 2021.

the degrees being granted. Our education system is geared towards skilling people for precisely the kind of work that is most likely to be automated. This situation is pervasive across most middle- and low-income countries in Africa, Asia and South America.

As you can see, the fast-changing nature of work has massive implications for all of us, which I will unpack in Chapter 7, but in a nutshell they are as follows:

- We need to quickly reframe our thinking away from jobs and employment to seeing ourselves as self-employed, freelancers and, if possible, as entrepreneurs.
- We must see work not as a job but as a series of projects. Sometimes you can have multiple 'projects' with one organization spanning years but don't fall into the trap of thinking this is a stable job. For more and more people, work is likely to resemble an evolving portfolio of projects, some of which are paid, whilst others satisfy our needs for impact, creative expression or community.
- You compete with machines not by outrunning or outlearning them but by becoming more human, and by developing better social and leadership skills, greater creativity and complex problem-solving ability.
- Success lies in doing what you are uniquely good at and being excellent at it. The new world is very unforgiving towards mediocrity and commoditized talent; but equally, for a person with initiative and drive to succeed, the opportunities are infinite.

Question 2: What are the implications of living till you're nearly 100?

Human life expectancy has been increasing steadily (by about two years every decade) in many parts of the world especially in developed and middle-income countries. We all know many more people in their 80s and 90s but few of us have thought through the implications of this trend for us personally. In a thought-provoking book, Lynda Gratton and Andrew Scott explore some of the consequences of a 100-year life for individuals, for organizations and for society.[11] It is worth a read.

For much of the last hundred years, people have been living a three-stage life where we spend the first 20 years learning, the next 40 earning and the final 10 or so years retiring to enjoy life and give back something to the world. If we live into our 80s or 90s, the three-stage life breaks down. Even in developed economies, many people will need to work till they are in their 70s or even 80s out of financial necessity; few can afford to stop earning by 60 and live off their savings. Most governments will not be able to fund their pension and social security schemes to support people living into their 90s. Many of us will also want to live engaging and productive lives as long as we can. To retire at 60 and spend 30 years vacationing would be both boring and unhealthy. But how many companies would be keen to employ a 70-year-old person in a world where 40 is already the new 60? So, what are we supposed to do as we get

---

[11]Lynda Gratton and Andrew Scott, *The 100-Year Life: Living and Working in an Age of Longevity,* Bloomsbury Information; 1st edition (2016).

older? How do we stay engaged? How do we financially support ourselves?

The second challenge of longevity is staying current in a world where the half-life of knowledge and skills is declining. In many engineering disciplines, the half-life of knowledge is already five years or less. As we get older, the pressure to learn new skills grows higher because we are competing against robots as well as younger generations even as our natural ability to learn changes. In my case, I observe that with age, I am getting better and better at pattern recognition and connecting the dots. While I have better judgment, my memory, my once-excellent facility with numbers and my capacity for detail have eroded. Of course, I keep challenging and pushing myself to learn new things by taking online courses, reading books, watching videos and picking up a new language—all of which slow down the process of mental ageing; yet, on many of the dimensions that employers look for, I would still be likely to lose out to a younger rival. There is a lot of glib talk about how learning doesn't stop with graduation and has to be lifelong. The fact, however, is that no companies, individuals or educational institutions are as yet geared for this.

So, increasingly, we have to shift our thinking from a traditional three-stage life to a multistage life where we must integrate learning, earning and enjoyment seamlessly. Work will increasingly be a dynamic portfolio of projects, some of which are paid but others that provide satisfaction, learning or are simply necessary. While there is growing discussion about how governments, society, employers and educational institutions will need to respond to this trend, I prefer to focus on what we can do as individuals.

The best advice on this comes from Lynda Gratton, who suggests building four different types of assets that are critical if we are to make the many seamless transitions that are part of a long, multistage life.[12] Financial assets which include savings, our home and possessions, are obviously, very important. But she emphasizes the critical importance of building intangible assets that include our skills, reputation, networks, self-knowledge, character, health and good relationships. So does my friend, Nipun Mehta of ServiceSpace, who has a terrific TED talk on multiple forms of wealth.[13]

Think of intangible assets as the things that enable us to stay both relevant and portable over time. The notion of portability is important. In the real world, what makes us portable or mobile? Well, it includes your identity documents (passport, driver's licence, Aadhaar or social security number), bank account and credit cards, your cell phone and Internet access. With these things, you can move about. Without them, you are stranded. The intangible assets serve the same purpose. They make you portable. They help you navigate change and transitions. Very few of us intentionally cultivate our intangible assets with the kind of focus we give to our tangible, financial assets. That is a big mistake.

---

[12]Ibid.

[13]Nipun Mehta, 'Unlocking Multiple Forms of Wealth', *Daily Good*, 19 April 2016, http://www.dailygood.org/story/1260/unlocking-multiple-forms-of-wealth-nipun-mehta. Accessed on 19 September 2021.

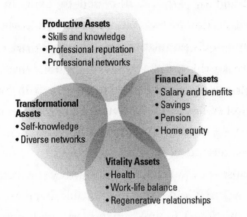

Productive Assets
• Skills and knowledge
• Professional reputation
• Professional networks

Financial Assets
• Salary and benefits
• Savings
• Pension
• Home equity

Transformational Assets
• Self-knowledge
• Diverse networks

Vitality Assets
• Health
• Work-life balance
• Regenerative relationships

Source: Lynda Gratton and Andrew Scott, *The 100-Year Life,* 2016.

Question 3: Could chaos engulf the place where you live?

My third question may seem like a really bizarre one especially if you live in a stable, democratic country like India or the US. When I speak to my family, friends and colleagues, the notion of societal collapse seems like the farthest thought on their minds. It is something that might happen in Afghanistan, Venezuela or Myanmar but not here. Yet, it is a scenario worth thinking about given what is going on around us.

Societal collapse is a rapid collapse of law and order, prosperity and population in a society. Public services and social cohesion crumble and chaos ensues as the government loses its monopoly on controlling violence. If you have trouble visualizing this, think about Syria or Iraq. So many once-great civilizations and empires no longer exist; they imploded. The Roman Empire covered 4.4 million square kilometres in 390 CE. In just five years, it shrank to 2 million square kilometres, and by 476 CE, it ceased to exist. In 1913, the mighty British Empire was at its peak and covered 23 per cent of the world's population and almost 24 per cent of the world's land area. Greatly weakened by the two World Wars, Britain began decolonizing starting with India in 1947. In just 20 years, most of her former colonies had gained independence and the sun set on the Empire. Germany took just 12 years to collapse after the Nazis came to power.

Is collapse just an artefact of history or could it, will it, happen again? Could the unthinkable happen to us? The collapse of the Soviet Union which began with unrest in some republics in 1988 was both recent and dramatic. In just three years, on Christmas Day 1991, the Soviet flag was lowered for the last time. No one could have imagined that the immensely powerful Soviet Union would simply implode into chaos. But it did. The collapse of prosperous Syria after the Arab Spring was even more dramatic with catastrophic consequences.

What causes a country or society to collapse?[14] Historians, sociologists and scientists point to several factors:

i.   Severe climate change that results in droughts, desertification and crop failure can trigger starvation, conflict and mass migration.

ii. Collapse can occur when societies overshoot the carrying capacity of their environment due to excessive deforestation, water pollution, soil degradation and the loss of biodiversity.

---

[14]Branko Milanovic, 'The Real Pandemic Danger Is Social Collapse', *Foreign Affairs*, 19 March 2020, https://www.foreignaffairs.com/articles/2020-03-19/real-pandemic-danger-social-collapse. Accessed on 19 September 2021.

iii. Pandemics have caused societies to collapse many times in history.

iv. A country can fail when the political system is captured by a group whose aim is to enrich and maximize its own welfare at the expense of everyone else. The state then turns predatory and preys increasingly on its businesses and citizens. All the wealth gets appropriated by a relatively small elite, corruption overwhelms society and, eventually, rule of law breaks down. There is a high risk of these conditions reaching a tipping point in many countries including middle-income democracies like Mexico, Nigeria, South Africa and India.

But the most important factor is the loss of social resilience, which is a society's ability to cooperate and act collectively for common goals. Extreme centralization of power and wealth and intentional polarization can cause trust and communication to break down. Today, we see greater polarization along religious, racial and ethnic lines, stoked by authoritarian leaders and fanned by social media, in many parts of the world.

People are then unable to cooperate and act collectively towards common goals, and so social, economic and ecological problems that could have been solved become bigger. As dissatisfaction and unrest grow among the citizens, power is used to suppress them. This then stokes resentment, fear, hate and violence. Syria is a perfect example of this. There, simmering discontent with the government resulted in major protests in the Arab Spring of 2011. The protests were brutally suppressed, resulting in a civil war that has destroyed an ancient, prosperous country and turned half its population into migrants and refugees.

I find this idea of social resilience—the ability of a group to cooperate and solve problems for the collective good—profoundly important. Both the countries I consider home—India and the US—have lost a lot of their ability to cooperate and solve problems with known solutions. (Take gun control or tax reform for instance in the US or almost any major policy reform in India.) Why is this happening? The simple answer is the loss of trust in our leaders, institutions and systems. But why has there been such a rapid erosion of trust concurrently in so many parts of the world?

Sociologist Zygmunt Bauman has written about the massive shift in beliefs, values, identities, relationships and global economics in contemporary society. He calls this phenomenon liquid modernity, a sensation of all that was solid and dependable turning fluid and becoming a turbulent current sweeping us all away.[15] Events unfold at a rate faster than we can comprehend and make sense of. This is intensely disorienting. According to Bauman, when uncertainty is the only certainty, when change is the only permanence, where ideas, beliefs and ethics are in flux, when decent, secure work is hard to come by, and social nets are fraying, constructing a durable identity for oneself becomes increasingly impossible. This results in huge numbers of people feeling disoriented, alienated, anxious, depressed, exploited and angry. In contemporary times, mental health issues are exploding. Masses of unmoored, anxious people in a world full of easy temptations, false heroes, polarizing leaders and fake narratives can unleash events that have huge repercussions for individuals and for the world.

---

[15]Zygmunt Bauman, *Liquid Modernity*, Wiley, 2000.

So, what is my point? It is that we are reaching a point where the unthinkable can happen—when perhaps not a whole country but a region or city can collapse into chaos. Many parts of Mexico, Nigeria and some parts of India are getting dangerously close to this point. The unprecedented mob attack on the US Capitol on 6 January 2021, allegedly egged on by a sitting president, indicates that this can happen almost anywhere.[16]

When that happens, you do not want to be there. The crucial point is to develop a set of tools that help you navigate the chaos and anchors that help you to stay oriented. This idea will be elaborated on in Chapter 5.

BLACK SWANS AND GREY RHINOS

If you have stayed with me this far, you probably have two important questions.

First of all, is it really all gloom and doom? Is the sky really falling? Isn't this what pessimists have been predicting for decades or even centuries?

In his bestselling book *The Black Swan*, Nassim Nicholas Taleb used the term 'black swan' to define improbable, unforeseeable events which have a massive impact on the world and seem obvious in hindsight.[17] One such event is the Great

---

[16]Lauren Leatherby, Arielle Ray, Anjali Singhvi, Christiaan Triebert, Derek Watkins and Haley Willis, 'How a Presidential Rally Turned Into a Capitol Rampage' *The New York Times*, 12 January 2021, https://www.nytimes.com/interactive/2021/01/12/us/capitol-mob-timeline.html. Accessed on 19 September 2021.

[17]Nassim Nicholas Taleb, *The Black Swan: The Impact of the Highly Improbable*, Penguin, 2008.

Depression of 1929 which caused 89 per cent of stock market wealth to be wiped out; the market didn't recover till 1950. During that period, the birth rate in America declined by 17 per cent, the divorce rate rose by a third and suicides rose by a half. There were few indicators in the years or even months leading up to the Depression of an event of this magnitude.

These days, there is another metaphor for risk, the grey rhino, which is used to describe a danger that is obvious and probable, but slow-moving and, therefore, conveniently ignored until it is too late. The climate crisis is the perfect example of an impending, slowly unfolding catastrophe which everyone is aware of but is being ignored by most. The COVID-19 pandemic is a classic grey rhino rather than a black swan; virologists and public health experts were amongst many who had been warning of an impending pandemic for years, but we conveniently ignored their warnings. We could have been much better prepared for the disaster.

The threats which I have described—of the impact of technological change, particularly of AI, of the enormous consequences of longevity and the dangers of societal collapse—are all grey rhinos. It is entirely possible that the rhino may ignore you and that you will be fine, but the consequences, if it does not, are so horrific that it is worth taking precautions. Everything is fine until it isn't. It is simply not worth ignoring these massive trends in the hope that things will turn out well eventually. Hope is not a strategy. What is needed is preparation. Chance favours the prepared mind. This is what the rest of the book is about.

AN ADAPTIVE CHALLENGE: ADAPT OR PERISH

The second question you might have is, 'Let us say these are plausible scenarios. What can *I* do to flourish in the midst of so much change and turbulence?'

I began this chapter with Charles Darwin's statement that periods of extreme and rapid change pose an adaptive threat; those who cannot adapt, suffer or perish, while those who do adapt, flourish. We are likely headed into such a binary and unforgiving world. However, while the world is turbulent and unforgiving, it is also filled with unprecedented opportunities for anyone with the right mindset and preparation. It is entirely possible to live well and flourish in a world that feels like it is falling apart. There is no contradiction in this.

The most important thing to remember is: *be intentional.* Don't just be like a piece of driftwood being carried around by life; that will probably not end well. Too many people live like barnacles, cautioned the writer John Gardner during a speech in 1990, stating, 'The barnacle is confronted with an existential decision about where it is going to live. Once it decides, it spends the rest of its life with its head cemented to a rock.'[18] Too many of us live like this, overwhelmed by complexity, exhausted by life's challenges, pulled down by victimhood and running out of steam somewhere along the way—a life wasted. As the renowned business executive Jack Welch said so well, 'Control your destiny or someone else will.'

---

[18]John Gardner, 'Personal Renewal'. A speech delivered to McKinsey & Company, Phoenix, Arizona on 10 November 1990. Available online at https://www.pbs.org/johngardner/sections/writings_speech_1.html. Accessed on 19 September 2021.

This book is meant to get you to think about some of the building blocks of an intentional life. What truly determines how we manifest in the world, what we achieve, whether we live a happy, largely satisfied life, is our mindset. So, I start with this in Chapter 2, 'Mindset: Your App for Life'. What are the assumptions that you have about yourself, who you are and what you are capable of? What are your assumptions about what success and failure are? What are your assumptions about other people and how the world works? How are these self-fulfilling? How are they limiting you and how can you reprogramme them? These are some of the issues addressed in this chapter.

What are the most foundational skills you will need in order to flourish in this century? Which skills are likely to become more valuable rather than obsolete? How do you compete with AI that is becoming ever more capable? These are questions that form the basis of the third chapter, 'Three Meta-Skills for the Age of AI'.

Our world is facing a huge number of challenges at every level—local, national and global. Climate change is the most existential threat to us. We have the means and the knowhow to address most of these but we are desperately lacking leadership. In the twenty-first century, leadership will most likely have to come from many of us—ordinary people doing extraordinary things—rather than primarily from those with title, power and wealth. So, we each have an opportunity to step up and lead. This is not just a moral imperative, a call to duty, but such leadership is key to finding meaning and satisfaction in life. These ideas are developed in Chapter 4, 'Be the Change'.

Chapter 5, 'Your GPS to Navigate a Chaotic World', offers

practical approaches to navigate an increasingly perilous world filled with easy temptations, dangerous leaders, fake news, lies and false narratives.

Money is a big challenge for most people. That is because, like salt, too little money or too much are both problematic. Chapter 6 is self-evidently titled, 'How Much Is Enough?'

In the twenty-first century, it is critical to think very differently about work. The idea of a stable 9–5 job with a salary and benefits is a rapidly fading one. While a predictable career may still be relevant for a tiny minority of people, most of us will be better off thinking of ourselves as freelancers or self-employed if not entrepreneurs. This may not be a comfortable thought but many more of us will be compelled to think and act this way. The good news is that once you do adapt, it is liberating and not scary. Going forward, it makes much more sense to figure out what makes your life meaningful and what you are good at and find a way to get paid for it, rather than the other way around. 'Do the best you can with what you're best at,' says writer Charles Handy[19] and I would merely add 'and get paid for it!' How you can join the 'passion economy' is a big part of Chapter 7, 'Navigate Your Career', where I share some practical suggestions on how to approach your work life.

As we try to compose our life in these extraordinary times, where everything stable around us seems to be melting and where events are unfolding at breakneck speed, how do we stay sane and deal with all the change? The solution lies in being anchored in your beliefs, your values, your commitments and

---

[19]Charles Handy, *21 Letters on Life and Its Challenges*, Random House UK, 2019.

in your relationships. The solution lies in learning to control your minds and reactions/responses to situations. The solution lies in feeling connected to and losing yourself in something bigger than yourselves. 'We are not human beings having a spiritual experience; we are spiritual beings having a human experience,' as Pierre Teilhard de Chardin, an influential Jesuit priest, said.

Our spirituality keeps us anchored in a turbulent world by helping us feel connected to the moment, to nature, to ourselves and to others. Spirituality is essential to make sense of whatever life serves up, particularly challenging and unpleasant experiences. It is central to redefining how you think of your self (your identity), measure your life and define success. I describe my own search for meaning in the eighth and final chapter, 'Reflecting on Success and Happiness'.

THE BEST OF TIMES, THE WORST OF TIMES

It was the best of times, it was the worst of times, it was the age of wisdom, it was the age of foolishness, it was the epoch of belief, it was the epoch of incredulity, it was the season of Light, it was the season of Darkness, it was the spring of hope, it was the winter of despair, we had everything before us, we had nothing before us, we were all going direct to Heaven, we were all going direct the other way.[20]

Many of you will recognize the opening lines of Charles

---

[20]Charles Dickens, *A Tale of Two Cities: A Story of the French Revolution*, Penguin Classics, 2003.

Dickens's *A Tale of Two Cities,* written in 1859. His description of the times continues to resonate even today, so perhaps, the world has always felt this way—at a tipping point in a tug of war between good and bad, hope and despair.

It is one thing to be aware of the big trends that are shaping our lives, but there is a great risk of becoming pessimistic. That is the wrong takeaway! Extreme change and shocks can be brutal if you don't have a reasonable measure of self-belief, initiative and grit. Ask yourself whether you would have been happier if you lived 50 years ago. Would you rather be a young person now or in some previous era? Sure, there are big problems and challenges with our world, but when I look at the immense possibilities and opportunities, the amazing things that many people—especially young people—are doing all over the world, I feel jealous!

I don't think there has ever been a better time to be alive. We are limited in what we can do with our lives only by our imagination and mindset. You can live an extraordinary life and make a great difference even if much of the world is a mess.

KEY IDEAS

The twenty-first century is likely to be a period of extreme change driven by many factors, including technology, climate change, demographics, inequality and polarization. Periods of extreme change create an adaptive challenge for all of us; those who can adapt to a VUCA world will flourish. Those who are unable to may suffer greatly.

The key to success is to live life more intentionally rather than simply being carried along like a piece of driftwood. Coping with extreme change requires us to develop a set of anchors that prevents us from being swept away. These anchors are our beliefs, commitments, important relationships and spirituality.

Despite the challenges, the twenty-first century is a time of unprecedented opportunities for anyone with the mindset of an explorer and the skill set of a change-maker. It is a time for optimism, not pessimism.

QUESTIONS FOR REFLECTION

1. List a few of the big trends that will or are influencing your life. For instance, longer life expectancy, advancement in technology and climate change. Is each of these trends a headwind or tailwind for you?
2. To what extent have you been intentional about your choices around where you live, what you do, who you hang out with and the kind of person you are?
3. How effectively have you built intangible assets like your reputation, networks, self-awareness, character and skills?
4. What are the critical questions that you hope to develop answers for, by the end of the book?

Mindset: Your App for Life

'What you believe affects what you achieve.'
—Bill Gates

∽

Why do some fairly ordinary people achieve so much in their life? Is it a matter of talent or of luck? Why do so many extremely talented people achieve so little? Why are so many successful people not happy? Why do smart people arrive at such different conclusions from the same facts? How are some people able to deal with extreme adversity with such grace, while others fall apart so quickly?

The answer to these questions has a lot to do with our mind and our mindset, which is the set of beliefs, assumptions and stories that we have about everything—about ourselves, others and life and how the world works. Think of your mindset as the software that runs your life; it determines how you manifest and interact with others. It determines how you define who you are, how you measure success and, therefore, what you do with your life and what you achieve. It determines how you deal with crises and your capacity for happiness. What you consider to be your reality is a manifestation of your mindset. The wonderful thing is that, like software, you can reprogramme your mindset and thereby change your reality.

This is probably the biggest personal insight that I have had in a decade and it is bringing about life-altering consequences.

BELIEVING IS SEEING

In Indian folklore, there is a story about a man who saw a big bull elephant tethered to a tree by a small rope tied to his leg. He was amazed that although the elephant could easily snap the rope and go free, it made no attempt to do this. The mahout explained that when the animals are very young, they are tied by the same rope and at that age, they are unable to break free. As they grow up, they are conditioned to believe that they still cannot.

What applies to elephants, applies to us as well. As Henry Ford said, 'Whether you think you can, or you think you can't—you're right.' Our beliefs shape our reality. The old proverb, 'seeing is believing', is actually wrong. I believe the opposite to be true—believing is seeing. What we believe is what manifests and becomes our reality.

DIGITAL TWINS

These days, there is great excitement in the tech world about digital twins. A digital twin is a detailed software model of a physical system like an aircraft or a power plant. Engineers can use the model to predict how the system will behave in the real world, optimize it, predict and prevent problems and so on.

The epiphany I have had is that our mind creates a twin of our world. We live not in the real world but in a model of the world that is created by our mind. This is not a new insight; it is just that I finally and truly got it.

When we 'see' a rose, what we are actually seeing is an image generated by our retina (sensor) by photons that bounce off the rose and enter the eye. We then decide that it is a rose and whether the rose is pretty or fading, based on a model we have of how a rose in bloom ought to look. This then triggers other thoughts and feelings; for instance, the thought, 'How dare he give me a wilted rose!' All of it is happening in the mind, so it turns out that we live not in the real world but in a model of the world that is synthesized by our mind. We experience the world through five sensors (senses) that are hooked up to our mind and that results in this incredible but virtual reality which we call our life. In particular, there is a disproportionately large part of our brain called the prefrontal cortex, which gives us the uniquely human capacity to imagine, build virtual prototypes, predict future outcomes, decide good and bad, set goals, plan and orchestrate our action in accordance with these goals. It is also responsible for social control, which is the ability to suppress urges that, if not suppressed, could lead to socially unacceptable outcomes. Most crucially, the seat of our ego—the 'I who is separate from everyone and everything else'—lies in the prefrontal cortex.

By changing the 'software' of our prefrontal cortex, we can change our assumptions, our goals and therefore our behaviour and life. Across different cultures there is an ancient wisdom that says, 'Nothing is as it is; everything is as we are', meaning that there is little that is objectively true, everything is subjective, and as 'seen' through the mind of the beholder. Now we are beginning to understand why. Even the great quantum physicist Werner Heisenberg pointed out that 'what we observe is not nature itself, but nature exposed to our method of questioning'.

The fact is simply that our mindset or beliefs shape what we want, whether we succeed in getting it and how we respond to various situations in life. It, therefore, shapes our life. By reprogramming our beliefs, we can reshape our life.

BELIEFS THAT ARE PARTICULARLY IMPORTANT

We have a nearly infinite number of beliefs or assumptions about everything conceivable including ourselves, other people, the world and how it works. I have found that some of our beliefs impact our life much more than others and therefore really worth focusing on. Here are a few of them:

1. Self-belief

Self-belief is a positive belief in our ability to set and achieve our goals in life. Beliefs are self-fulfilling; judging yourself to be capable of something vastly increases your chance of success and vice versa. 'I want to study at Harvard and I believe I am good enough to get there', 'I am 60 but I can still get a master's degree in Data Science and run a marathon', 'I won't be applying for that job because I don't think I have what it takes', 'It's not too late for me to become an entrepreneur and be successful at it,' or 'I am ugly; who would ever love me?'—all these are examples of beliefs that we subconsciously have of ourselves.

Like the elephant in the story, how many of us go through life hanging onto the belief that we cannot do something, simply because we failed at it once before? How many of us are being held back by old, outdated beliefs that no longer serve us? How many of us have avoided trying something new because of a limiting belief? How many of us are being held back by someone else's limiting beliefs about us?

Self-belief is highly correlated with self-esteem. The good news is that both can be developed and also rebuilt if damaged. The key is to recognize some of the self-limiting beliefs that are dramatically holding us back. There are lots of resources that can be helpful in overcoming self-doubt.[21] What I have personally found quite helpful are these five techniques:

i.   Confront your inner critic: Do it with data that proves you are capable. If you don't think you are successful, write down 10 facts that prove otherwise.

ii.   Lean into your fears: Fears are definitionally irrational. When you confront them, they tend to evaporate. When I was a child, I was afraid of ghosts and dark rooms; by sitting alone in a dark room one evening, I overcame that fear. Later in life, I had a fear that if I were not the CEO of some important company, I would not matter to anyone. By getting off the CEO treadmill and realizing that it did not matter to those who I care about, I have managed to overcome that mindset.

iii. Affirm and love yourself: If you are wracked with

---

[21] Jacqueline T. Hill, 'How to Develop Self-Belief in 8 Steps', *Lifehack*, 14 December 2020, https://www.lifehack.org/871375/self-belief. Accessed on 22 November 2021.

self-doubt, simply writing down and recalling all the good qualities you have on a daily basis, can really help. So can getting feedback from people who matter to you.

iv. Cut off negative people: Simply walk away from people who erode your self-esteem and self-confidence.

v. Encourage others to pursue their dreams: This is a wonderful counter-intuitive tool. When you encourage and affirm others, you feel affirmed. A little bit of fragrance clings to the hand that gives the rose.

2. Agency and personal responsibility

Agency is the belief that *you* are in charge of your life. Your life is not controlled by planets, fate, your manager, your parents or spouse. You are the one making choices and decisions and accept responsibility for these. You are not a victim. If you do not like your circumstances, you can make changes.

Like many others, I was very reactive. If someone was mean to me, it would ruin my day and I would make sure to spoil it for others too. If I did not feel successful enough, I needed to find someone to blame for it, thereby becoming the victim. What changed my perspective was Stephen R. Covey's bestselling book, *The 7 Habits of Highly Effective People*, where he defined responsibility as 'response-ability'.[22] That is, the ability to choose one's response to any situation or circumstance. If you do not like your circumstances, then take the onus of making the changes that improve them. Don't look for someone to blame. Becoming an adult is learning to take personal responsibility for your life. Not only is the idea

---

[22]Stephen R. Covey, *The 7 Habits of Highly Effective People*, Mango, 2016.

of agency extremely empowering, it is the foundation of all achievement and satisfaction in life.

3. The growth mindset

Psychologist Carol Dweck draws a distinction between two internally consistent set of beliefs which she calls the 'fixed mindset' versus a 'growth mindset'.[23] People with a fixed mindset have a fundamental belief in nature rather than nurture; they believe that the attributes that matter such as intelligence, talent, personality and character are what you are born with. Success means showing you have plenty of these, which leads to a tendency to want to always be the smartest person in the room—the know-it-all, the precocious genius. Effort is for the less talented. Failure is a problem because it shows you are incompetent. Therefore, failure is something you must avoid at all costs, which means playing it safe and never taking on big challenges. When people inevitably encounter failure or setback, it is devastating because it affects their identity and self-worth. Feedback is criticism. The locus of control of their life is outside them; when things don't go their way, they are a victim and need to find someone to blame. The success of others results in jealousy and feelings of inadequacy. Therefore, they have a consuming goal of proving themselves—in the classroom, in their careers and in their relationships. Every situation calls for a confirmation of their intelligence, personality or character. Every situation is evaluated by asking questions like: 'Will I succeed or fail?', 'Will I come across as smart or dumb?', 'Will I be accepted or rejected?' and 'Will I feel like a winner or a loser?'

---

[23]Carol S. Dweck, *Mindset: The New Psychology of Success*, Random House; Illustrated edition (2006).

Dweck then goes on to show that there is a very different set of beliefs that she calls a 'growth mindset'. People with a growth mindset have a central belief that what you are born with is just the starting point for development and that your capabilities and character are developed through a lifetime of intentional effort. The growth mindset creates a powerful passion for learning, the desire to 'learn it all versus know it all'. Setbacks are seen as an inevitable part of learning; the only failure is giving up in the face of obstacles. Feedback is critical for learning and personal responsibility is crucial for success. The success of others inspires admiration and emulation rather than envy. 'Why waste time proving over and over how great you are,' Dweck writes, 'when you could be getting better? Why hide deficiencies instead of overcoming them? Why look for friends who will just shore up your self-esteem instead of ones who will also challenge you to grow? And why seek out the tried and true, instead of experiences that will stretch you?'[24]

A central difference between a growth mindset and a fixed mindset is what we think about failure. To a person with a growth mindset, setbacks are different from failure. They are temporary obstacles which only means that you need to try harder to find a way around or through them. The only failure is giving up. Quitting. They would fully agree with Winston Churchill, who said, 'Success is not final, failure is not fatal: it is the courage to continue that counts.' Think about a small child learning to walk; she wobbles and falls a hundred times before finally being able to take the first

---

[24]Ibid.

faltering steps. What would happen if she gave up after the first two times she fell?

Dweck sums up by saying, 'Out of these two mindsets, which we manifest from a very early age, springs a great deal of our behaviour, our relationship with success and failure and ultimately our capacity for happiness.'[25] As you might have guessed by now, the growth mindset is what will allow you to overcome the most challenging moments of your life and thrive in the VUCA world that we are living in.

4. Abundance

Covey coined the distinction between an abundance mindset and a scarcity mentality. Scarcity mentality refers to seeing everything in life as a small and finite pie, so if one person takes a piece, that leaves less for you. An abundance mindset refers to the belief that there is plenty out there for everybody. Scarcity and abundance have nothing to do with what you actually have; they have everything to do with how you feel about what you have. A beggar who joyously offers to buy you a cup of tea has an abundance mindset. A billionaire who skips town to avoid a meeting where he might be asked to support some cause has a scarcity mindset. (Both are true stories!)

Abundance and scarcity apply not just to money. Nipun Mehta helped me understand that there are many forms of wealth and therefore many forms of poverty. Precious assets include money, time, information, expertise, networks and love. You could have an abundance mindset around money and a scarcity mindset around time or love.

---

[25]Carol S. Dweck, *Mindset: The New Psychology of Success*, Ballantine Books; Updated Edition, 2007.

A scarcity mindset makes us obsessed about things and we start hoarding them. Our thinking becomes short term and all this gets in the way of achieving our true potential. Scarcity makes us obsess over resources rather than a purpose and outcomes. Abundance thinking makes us smarter. In one famous experiment, scientists gave a group of farmers an Intelligence Quotient (IQ) test before the harvest and then the same test after a good harvest. Their average IQ scores improved by 13 points after the harvest. The same test was repeated with the same farmers. The difference is that post-harvest, they were less worried about money.

An abundance mindset can and must be cultivated. There are simple but highly effective techniques to do this; for instance:

i.   Catch yourself and become aware of where and when you have a scarcity mentality. Try to remind yourself of how much you actually have.

ii.   Practise gratitude. Every morning, start the day by counting all your blessings and good fortune and feel grateful for this abundance.

iii.   Be in the company of people who have an abundance mindset such as people who are positive and see the glass always half-full. Abundance and scarcity are both contagious.

iv.   Focus more on goals and possibilities rather than resources and constraints. As Gandhi famously said, 'Find purpose. The means will follow.' Ask yourself what would you do if money, time, etc., were not constraints. Commit yourself to that and the rest will follow.

5. The big questions

The 'big questions' are the eternal ones like:

i. 'Who am I?'
ii. 'Why am I here?'
iii. 'What will make me happy?'
iv. 'Why do bad things happen to good people like me?'

These are the central questions in life and in the realm of philosophy and spirituality. Our implicit assumptions about these questions determine much of what happens to us—what we accomplish, how we deal with whatever happens to us, and how we feel about ourselves and our life. So, these are *the* most fundamentally important beliefs we have. Unfortunately, very few of us have intentionally shaped our beliefs about these questions. Usually, our beliefs develop through a subconscious process of agglomeration as we go through life, and there are a lot of viruses and malware in these. This has enormous consequences.

Take success, for example. If we define success in financial terms, that is what we will pursue, with all its consequences— good and bad. If having a million followers on Twitter is what you believe to be a proxy for success, you will waste many hours a day tweeting, often making inane or provocative comments and getting sucked into pointless arguments like so many otherwise accomplished people I know, do. If you define it in terms of being in service of others, your life will take on a very different complexion, with different outcomes.

What is your belief around happiness? For many of us, it is 'I will be happy *only* if I get X.' X is always something we do not have and is a moving target. It can be a good grade, a lucrative job, a raise, a promotion, finding love, a better house or a vacation in Hawaii. Happiness, then, is a moving goalpost, indefinitely postponed. For others, happiness is simply a state of mind that you cultivate and is quite independent of external circumstances.

As you might imagine, these existential questions are amongst the deepest and most difficult to answer. Some psychologists like Viktor Frankl see our entire life as a quest for meaning, as a search for the answers to some of these questions.[26] Because the questions are uncomfortable, and the process of answering them is so difficult, many of us, like me, postpone thinking about them for a later stage in life until they become impossible to ignore. If you are lucky, you might be able to get away with this. But given the extreme fluidity and turbulence of our times, I think it is important to start becoming intentional about these questions now, whether you are young or older.

Historian Yuval Noah Harari says that we each need a compelling positive narrative that we believe in.[27] This helps us stay sane when things around us are not. For some of us, the story is religion. But religion does not necessarily mean believing in a God who created our world and rules over us. It is belief in a story that provides some explanation for the way things are, along with a system of values and norms. Buddhists believe in the natural laws of karma and a Noble Eightfold Path to stay centred. Devout Christians believe in a Day of Judgment, when God will manifest and save us—at least the

[26]Viktor E. Frankl, *Man's Search for Meaning: The Classic Tribute to Hope from the Holocaust*, RHUK; Exported edition (2008).
[27]Yuval Noah Harari, *Sapiens: A Brief History of Humankind*, Penguin Random House; 1st edition (2015).

devout amongst us. Followers of Vedanta believe there is no 'I' which is separate from everything else and that everything is transient and illusory. Silicon Valley technologists have their own religion; they believe technological progress will save us from the mess that we have created.

The validity or truth behind these narratives is unknown and unknowable, but it may not matter as much as our conviction. When things around us feel overwhelming, we need a robust and positive belief system to sustain us and to provide some stability to our life.

MINDSET IS REPROGRAMMABLE

From time to time, we find ourself in a really difficult situation with lots of stress, suffering and unhappiness. Despite our efforts to make things better, the situation becomes chronic and fails to be resolved. Sometimes there is a pattern; we repeatedly find ourselves in a similar circumstance. The advice of well-intentioned friends and colleagues seems reasonable but hard to implement. So does the advice of self-help books and videos that we so avidly read and watch, respectively. It's like water off a duck's back. Very little sticks. The suffering continues.

That is because while I may understand things intellectually, my basic mindset, my most fundamental beliefs and assumptions are telling me something else. For instance, let us take the success narrative. Let us say you are not feeling successful right now. Your best friend tells you, 'Ravi, you *are* successful. Look at the number of people who care about you and look up to you.' But if your fundamental measure of success is something very different—let us say it is about wealth, power, achievements and recognition—your friend's advice is simply meaningless. Unless you are able to change your definition of success, you are not going to feel better about yourself.

The beautiful thing is that you can reprogramme your assumptions and beliefs. And when you do, you change your reality. Motivational speaker Dr Wayne Dyer once said, 'When you change the way you see things, the things that you see change.' This is one of the most powerful and empowering ideas ever. Let me share a couple of personal examples in this context.

I was 25 when I became a team manager for the first time. It was in 1988, on the shop floor of a unionized American factory where the work ethic was poor. My team members felt that four hours was a good day's work. My only managerial role model till then had been my mother, who used to run a large home with a couple of maids and a gardener, among others. Her method of managing them would be to supervise them. This involved walking closely behind each of them, catching them doing something wrong and then criticizing them. I unconsciously ended up emulating her. I would spend all day on the floor watching my team and keeping an eagle eye, nagging and scolding them, and sometimes even chasing them out of the restroom if they were taking too long a break. I just hated my work, and I think they hated me. Something had to give.

Around that time, I read the outstanding, now-forgotten, *The Human Side of Enterprise* by Douglas McGregor.[28] McGregor proposed two alternative theories we hold about human motivation. Believers in Theory X, such as my mom,

---

[28]Douglas McGregor, *The Human Side of Enterprise*, McGraw-Hill Education, 2006.

held that most people have low ambition, are lazy and avoid responsibility. They, therefore, need continuous supervision, external rewards and consequences. McGregor proposed a better Theory Y, whose fundamental belief is that most people are internally motivated, to say, learn and take responsibility. Work should therefore be designed to allow a high degree of self-control and to be intrinsically satisfying. People need feedback and coaching more than supervision. The shoe dropped. I was clearly following Theory X. *Perhaps I should give Theory Y a shot.* I did. I began treating them as adults. We agreed on what would be acceptable performance in terms of output, quality and housekeeping. I began to teach them the basics of computer numerical control (CNC) programming. We went to other factories on learning tours. For five of my six operators, the results were excellent; only one of them was irredeemably lazy. When I applied to a business school two years later, the most glowing recommendation I got was from the union leader. Much of my professional success in managing even larger organizations goes back to this moment in 1990, when I finally changed my assumptions about human motivation.

Another, more difficult, shift was trying to be less pessimistic. It was not till I was about 40 that I realized that I was actually a chronic pessimist. I always thought poorly of the pessimists around me, and it came as a shock to realize that I was one myself. I knew I had to change for three reasons. First, optimists generally achieve more and are more successful than pessimists; it is rare to find a successful salesperson or entrepreneur who is a chronic pessimist. And I was determined to be successful. Second, no one likes to be around pessimists and negative people. Finally, optimists are happier people. But awareness is one thing, and change is quite another. Fortunately, my friend Steve Knaebel helped me see that pessimists have three fundamental beliefs; when something 'bad' happens, pessimists instinctively jump to three conclusions:

1. The worst possible outcome is what will happen.
2. It will last forever.
3. It is personal. Why is this happening to *me*?[29]

Optimists, on the other hand, know it is rarely personal; hopefully, it will not be as bad as one might fear, and in any case, this too shall pass. Steve taught me to catch myself, to become aware every time I found myself reacting pessimistically and then, consciously challenge the three assumptions. It took a few years for me to change significantly, but change, I did!

I know from experience that changing your beliefs and assumptions is not easy, but it is always possible. The hardest beliefs to change are naturally the most deep-rooted ones. In my case, they were my beliefs and narratives around success and happiness. In every case, change begins with awareness. Take for instance some aspect of your life that is creating stress or unhappiness and which is simply not getting better. For once, resist the temptation to externalize the cause. Instead, step back and ask yourself— 'How am I unconsciously contributing to this situation?' Ask yourself what assumptions you may be making about yourself, the other person, about success, about winning and losing. What can you change that might improve the situation? Then test this in practice and take your way forward. As you do this, you find yourself moving from conscious incompetence to a fragile

---

[29]Martin E.P. Seligman, *Learned Optimism: How to Change Your Mind and Your Life*, Vintage, 2006.

conscious competence before eventually, your new beliefs take root. In psychology, this evolution is known as the conscious competence learning model.

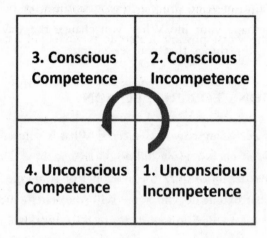

As mentioned earlier: 'Nothing is as it is. Everything is as we are.' Once you really understand this, life becomes better and better.

KEY IDEAS

1. Mindset is the software that runs your life. It is the set of beliefs, assumptions and stories that we have about everything—from ourselves, to how the world works. It determines how you manifest and interact with others. It determines what you do with your life and what you achieve. It determines how you deal with crises and your capacity for happiness.

2. Our beliefs about ourself, about the extent to which we are responsible for our life, about success and failure,

about abundance and about why we exist are particularly fundamental. It is worth examining these carefully and changing them where necessary.

3. Like any software, you can reprogramme your beliefs, you can reshape your life. When you change the way you see things, the things that you see change.

QUESTIONS FOR REFLECTION

1. What according to you is success? What is failure? Are you largely a success? How did you arrive at these definitions? Whose definitions are these—yours or someone else's?

2. To what extent do you agree with the statement, 'I am in charge of my decisions and choices?' To what extent do you believe your life is significantly influenced by other people (parents, spouse, manager, friend) or forces (the planets and stars, for instance)?

3. When you face a setback or severe challenge, do you simply focus on dealing with the situation or do you tend to blame other people or circumstances? Ask those around you for feedback.

4. What deep beliefs might you have about yourself that are limiting you?

5. Would those closest to you (friends, family, co-workers) say you mostly have a fixed or a growth mindset?

6. Would those closest to you say you mostly have an abundance or scarcity mindset about money, time, love and expertise?

7. What one or two beliefs must you change to unlock your life?

.3.

Three Meta-Skills for the Age of AI

*'The illiterate of the twenty-first century will not be those who
cannot read and write, but those who cannot learn,
unlearn and relearn.'*
—Alvin Toffler

∽

As I started thinking about this topic, I googled 'What skills do you need these days?' and it threw up 1.43 billion results! A similar query, 'What skills should I learn?' had 1.26 billion results. This does appear to be a question that is on many people's minds. The other interesting thing was the variety of answers that the searches threw up. They ranged from public speaking and writing to home repair, UX design, data science, sales, digital literacy, coding, meditation, learning to learn and creativity. A similar search on LinkedIn threw up a much smaller but equally diverse range of advice. It was not clear, however, how a person looking for real help in deciding what to learn could get any.

Life used to be simpler. For most part of the twentieth century, education, particularly higher education, was the ticket out of poverty. The Second Industrial Revolution powered by electricity needed a literate and numerate workforce. The computer age allowed those with training in science, technology and mathematics to do particularly well; I was lucky to be part of this wave. But the age of AI is upending all this. Higher education is no longer an assurance of a reasonable life. From Nigeria to India, young graduates and postgraduates are struggling to find employment. Many engineers and MBA graduates are being forced into parcel delivery or even manual labour. At the same time, more companies, including Google, IBM and Apple, are hiring more and more employees without a degree, provided they demonstrate certain skills and aptitude. Degrees are declining in value for good reason. The education system in most countries is designed for a world that is fast disappearing. It trains people in precisely those areas where computers are already much better than human beings.

At the same time, relevant skills do matter a lot. Employers all over the world are facing chronic talent shortages. In a survey of global CEOs in September 2020 by KPMG, talent risk has risen 11 places since the start of the pandemic, emerging as the greatest threat to businesses around the world, ahead of even supply chain and environmental risk.[30] A Korn Ferry survey of 1,500 chief experience officers (CXOs) has 68 per cent forecasting a shortage of talent. The talent shortage could cost firms nearly $8.5 trillion in lost revenue by 2030[31] and inflate

---

[30]KPMG 2020 CEO Outlook: COVID-19 Special Edition, KPMG, https://assets.kpmg/content/dam/kpmg/xx/pdf/2020/09/kpmg-2020-ceo-outlook.pdf. Accessed on 24 November 2021.
[31]Michael Franzino, Alan Guarino, Yannick Binvel and Jean-Marc Laouchez, 'The $8.5 Trillion Talent Shortage', *Korn Ferry*, https://www.kornferry.com/insights/this-week-in-leadership/talent-crunch-future-of-work. Accessed on 2 December 2021.

salaries by $2.5 trillion. This is not surprising when you consider that every organization—whether a small local store, a bank, a manufacturing company or a college—has to transform itself to survive. Every business is now a technology business and needs employees who understand things such as data analytics and digital marketing. What's hot changes quickly, and today's hot skills will be irrelevant tomorrow. So, companies need people who are adaptable, entrepreneurial and able to constantly learn new skills. This is where the real problem lies.

There simply aren't enough such people. Education systems are not designed to develop such talent, nor are most company training programmes. Effective career counselling services that help guide people down suitable pathways based on their aptitude and interest are few and far between. So, a very large number of people are now feeling lost. Unfortunately, in an unequal world with binary outcomes, for individuals without the relevant skills, the consequences can be catastrophic. So, in this chapter, I will focus on 'what to learn and how to learn it'.

WHAT TO LEARN: META-SKILLS

In a world where automation is like a rising tide that can do more and more of the tasks that humans perform, where new technologies are being invented every day, where new kinds of jobs and roles are springing into existence and once hot skills become quickly irrelevant or commoditized, what do you learn?

Your focus must be less on specific skills such as coding and more on 'meta-skills'. Meta-skills are higher-order, general skills that enable you to develop new skills. To use the metaphor of an iceberg, skills are like the tip of the iceberg that lies above the water, while meta-skills are the 90 per cent of the iceberg that lies below the water. For example, the gift of picking up new languages is a meta-skill. These skills are durable and will be valuable decades from now. While there are many meta-skills, from personal experience, I have found that four stand out. These are:

Meta-Skill 1: Learning Agility

Thirty years ago, Prof. Chris Argyris at Harvard University published a seminal article in the *Harvard Business Review* called 'Teaching Smart People How to Learn'.[32] He discovered that smart, accomplished graduates from institutions such as Harvard and Massachusetts Institute of Technology (MIT) who were hired because their employers assumed they were the best at learning, were not very good at it. These graduates were generally good at solving problems or updating their technical skills but were generally surprisingly poor at something Argyris calls 'double-loop learning'.

To understand the idea of double-loop learning, think about a simple room thermostat that automatically turns on the AC whenever the temperature goes above 25 degree Celsius. It is a good example of single-loop learning. A thermostat that can reason, 'Why am I set at 25 degrees?' and then explore whether or not some other temperature might be more optimal would be engaging in double-loop learning.

---

[32]Chris Argyris, 'Teaching Smart People How to Learn', *Harvard Business Review* (May–June 1991); https://hbr.org/1991/05/teaching-smart-people-how-to-learn. Accessed on 22 November 2021.

Smart people, Argyris found, were good at single-loop learning, that is, learning new facts, concepts and tools and applying them to solve problems. They tended to become experts in a narrow arena. But they tended to be quite poor at double-loop learning, i.e., where they would not just attempt to solve the problems presented to them but were able to sense the context and ask if these were even the right problems and question the implicit assumptions. A lot of left-brain thinkers are like this; they are fact-based, detail-oriented, and good at logical and analytical reasoning and mathematics. Many engineers, in particular, are trained to be this way.

One of the reasons why a lot of people are poor at double-loop learning is that they have a tendency to avoid failing and hence stay in a zone of comfort. Even when they fail, they struggle to introspect and grow from this experience, and as a result, they frequently plateau or fail in their careers.

Even 30 years ago, Argyris saw that as the environment grew more competitive, more turbulent and fast-paced, managers would need to get better at 'double-loop' learning. Today, these ideas have been subsumed into the concept of 'learning agility', a term that is increasingly used by HR professionals and psychologists to predict long-term success.

So, what is learning agility? What it's not is simple single-loop learning; for example, learning a new programming language such as Python or new tools for data analysis.

That is necessary but far from sufficient. Instead, learning agility is a person's ability to quickly size up a new situation or problem and decide what to do. It is the ability to quickly make sense of a new context; it is about pattern recognition. It is the ability to continually and rapidly learn, unlearn and relearn mental models and practices from a variety of experiences, people and sources, and to apply that learning in new and changing contexts to achieve results. In short, learning agility is about knowing what to do when you don't know what to do and it may be one of the strongest predictors of a person's ability to flourish in a VUCA world.

Learning agility has five major components:

i.   Mental agility, or how comfortable you feel dealing with new and complex tasks, how well you can see patterns and connect disparate dots.

ii. People agility, or how well you can work with others especially those who are different from you.

iii. Change agility, or how comfortable you feel with completely new experiences, ambiguity or change.

iv. Results agility, or whether you can remain positive and deliver results in crisis or fast-changing situations.

v.   Self-awareness, or how well you can recognize your strengths and weaknesses.

Learning-agile individuals are curious, have an open mind, enjoy taking on new and big challenges, learn quickly from experience, and can grasp new concepts and complex issues. They thrive in ambiguous, changing situations and are tenacious in the face of obstacles and setbacks. If it sounds similar to the growth mindset I had described earlier, it is because it is highly correlated.

So how do you develop learning agility? Learning agility cannot be learnt online or in a classroom. The only reliable way that I know, is through experience, by taking on new challenges and seeing them through to success. These experiences become 'crucibles' in which your self-confidence and learning agility get strengthened, much as you get fitter by regularly hitting the gymnasium.

I'll share my personal story here. I owe much of my professional success to one of my managers at Cummins. Joe Loughrey was the president of the company and was one of the best developers of talent that I know. He had an instinctive eye for latent potential, and his way of both testing and developing a person was to throw them a challenge that was much bigger than what they were ready for. I was lucky that I caught his attention. My first project straight after an MBA was to lead the rationalization of Cummins's global manufacturing operations. My small team was to help the management decide what operations to exit or close and where to invest for the future. This was an unstructured project and required me to interface with every part of the company and people at every level. I had to learn new things quickly, overcome considerable scepticism and hostility, and also learn to lead by influence rather than authority. It was an outstanding experience. Joe then packed me off to fix our chronically money-losing piston-ring business outside Atlanta. Here, I had to deal not only with an unproductive and poorly led workforce, but difficult race relations and even a scary brush with the Ku Klux Klan. My success here was rewarded with an even tougher job, which was to fix or close Cummins's failing joint venture in India with Tata Motors. This was a massive operation—much bigger and vastly more complex than anything I had handled before. I have a sneaking suspicion that I got this role only because no one else wanted it. How many capable managers would want to go live in Jamshedpur and try to fix a bleeding business that neither parent company cared about? Anyway, it turned out to be another fantastic opportunity and eventually resulted in Cummins's businesses in India becoming the crown jewel of the empire.

The point is this: thanks to sheer good luck, I worked for a terrific manager who intentionally threw me into successively bigger challenges; these became crucibles for my learning and development as a leader. Each new challenge pushed me completely out of my comfort zone. I had to rapidly learn new things to survive. This is how I developed learning agility, people and general management skills, and this is why, over time, I was able to successfully take on extremely diverse professional challenges across multiple industries and sectors.

I have used this approach to developing talent at other companies that I worked with, with considerable success. Many companies have a leadership development programme for high-potential talent. These are rarely effective and internal succession remains a big challenge. What works is conceptually incredibly simple. You create two lists. One is a list of the most difficult problems, and biggest opportunities the company or division of the company is facing and create missions and projects around these. The second is a list of the perceived high-potential talent across different levels of the organization. You then map this talent to the list of challenging, mission-critical projects. People have to stretch, learn and collaborate to achieve 'impossible' goals. The entire senior management gets involved in mentoring the projects and the talent. These challenging projects then become 'crucibles for leadership'; this is how you develop leaders in the company systematically, intentionally, transparently, and the output is business breakthroughs and a pipeline of leaders.

I call this process 'Hot People-Hot Jobs' and if taken seriously, it works 100 per cent of the time.

I also want to make a related point about generalists versus specialists. For a long while, specialization in some discipline or great expertise has been a reliable path to success. But it appears that in the future, generalists who have a broad range of interests and experiences and can turn on a dime and adapt to a new scenario have a big advantage. There is an excellent book, *Range*, by David Epstein if you want to delve deeper into this.[33] The mathematician Freeman Dyson used a nice metaphor stating, 'Some mathematicians are birds, others are frogs. Birds fly high in the air and survey broad vistas out to the far horizon. They delight in concepts that unify our thinking and bring together diverse problems from different parts of the landscape. Frogs live in the mud below and see only the flowers that grow nearby. They delight in the details of particular objects, and they solve problems one at a time.' The world needs both birds and frogs, specialists and generalists. But in an uncertain and fast-changing world, birds can find new habitats and food better than frogs. Generalists will have more opportunities and can adapt better to change.

Meta-Skill 2: Entrepreneurial Mindset and Skills

The twenty-first century will be a century of entrepreneurship. This will be driven by both opportunity and necessity. New technologies and inventions are creating extraordinary new business opportunities. Every major problem, such as climate

---

[33]David Epstein, *Range: Why Generalists Triumph in a Specialized World*, Riverhead Books, Illustrated edition, 2019.

change or plastic waste, also creates corresponding business opportunities in the emerging green economy. On the other hand, the shortage of stable jobs will force many more of us to become self-employed or 'necessity entrepreneurs'. A few of these necessity entrepreneurs will become very successful. Some of the greatest companies, such as General Motors, FedEx, Hewlett-Packard and International Business Machines (IBM), were born out of twentieth-century recessions.

But here is the *real* point. While not everyone will be an entrepreneur, every person will need to have an entrepreneurial mindset to flourish in the volatile and turbulent twenty-first century. The Network for Teaching Entrepreneurship (NFTE) defines an entrepreneurial mindset as a set of beliefs and skills that enable people to identify and make the most of opportunities, overcome and learn from setbacks, and succeed in a variety of settings.[34] Their research shows that an entrepreneurial mindset is highly valued by employers, boosts educational attainment and performance and is crucial for creating new businesses. The most important thing to remember is this: entrepreneurship is like any skill. You can learn it and get better at it with practise. Most entrepreneurs are made, not born.

What are some of the attributes of an entrepreneurial mindset, and how do you develop these? As usual, there are lots of factors correlated with successful entrepreneurs, but some of the top attributes are these:

    i.   They dream bigger. Like all successful people, entrepreneurs believe that they are in control of their

---

[34]'Entrepreneurial Mindset', NFTE, https://www.nfte.com/entrepreneurial-mindset/. Accessed on 22 November 2021.

choices and destiny. They can imagine a brighter future and have the determination to make it happen despite constraining circumstances. This is highly correlated with the attributes of self-determination and agency in psychology.

ii. They recognize opportunity. They have the positive and optimistic ability to see and experience problems as opportunities and to create solutions. The entrepreneur sees an opportunity in every problem, not the difficulty in every opportunity. In that respect, this time of great problems also represents a time of abundant opportunities. For instance, the so-called low-carbon 'green economy' is already worth $10 trillion and has enormous opportunities for small, local businesses, not just large ones. Many websites list ideas that range from composting to waste recycling, from second-hand stores to refilling ink cartridges. There is no shortage of opportunities in the world, just a shortage of entrepreneurs.

iii. They are persuasive. Most successful entrepreneurs are excellent storytellers. In the beginning, they have only an idea or a concept, but they need to be able to tell a compelling story to persuade the first employees, the first customers and the first funders to join or support their endeavour.

iv. They are resourceful. One of the best definitions of entrepreneurship that I have ever heard is that it is the relentless pursuit of opportunity without regard to resources currently controlled. Resourcefulness matters much more than resources. This is a central belief of all entrepreneurs.

v. They are problem-solvers and action-oriented. Successful entrepreneurs can consider an issue from a range of possible perspectives to come up with creative solutions. They 'move fast and break things', that is, they try many things to find a solution that works rather than get paralysed by overthinking.

vi. They are tenacious. The ability to tenaciously keep going, changing plans and actions, if necessary, to overcome challenges or even failure is utterly crucial.

Incidentally, you may notice that the attributes of entrepreneurship are similar to the attributes of leadership. This is no coincidence. You cannot be an entrepreneur if you are not a leader.

Entrepreneurship is a learnt mindset and skill set. One of the scholars of the subject is Professor Saras Sarasvathy of the Darden School of Business who terms this as 'effectuation', which refers to the lessons that experienced serial entrepreneurs learnt while building their ventures.[35] She found that serial entrepreneurs develop new ways of thinking and problem-solving by learning from their failures and successes. What they become good at is 'crossing the river by feeling their way across the stones.' This is something that can only be learnt from experience.

Much of my work these days involves working with aspiring entrepreneurs. We set up a non-profit organization called the

---

[35]Caroline Newman, 'Q&A: Darden Professor Cracks the Code of How Great Entrepreneurs Think', UVA Darden Ideas to Action, https://ideas.darden.virginia.edu/darden-professor-cracks-the-code-of-how-great-entrepreneurs-think, 2019. Accessed on 22 November 2021.

Global Alliance for Mass Entrepreneurship (GAME) to help create an entrepreneurial movement in India. As part of this, my co-founder Mekin Maheshwari has been involved in a fascinating experiment with the Government of Delhi to help young people across more than 1,000 government schools develop an entrepreneurial mindset. His team at Udhyam Foundation has developed and prototyped a curriculum to strengthen some of the entrepreneurial attributes I talked about. They do it through novel, experiential and team-based ways.

For instance, to teach grit, students are asked to make a paper plane with their non-dominant hand alone. They then reflect on what enabled some to succeed. Resourcefulness is learnt by working in groups to make the tallest possible tower using desks, bags, books, anything they can find, including standing on each other's shoulders. They are asked to read a news article, separate facts from opinions and then start a debate switching sides after five minutes; this develops critical thinking.

About 750,000 young people from the humblest socio-economic backgrounds have been going through this compulsory programme for about a year; the results in terms of self-confidence, morale and performance are impressive. Compelled by the pandemic, many youngsters have already started on their entrepreneurial journey. Monu Kumar, a twelfth-grade student, repairs electric rickshaws after school to support his family. He dreams of starting a big repair business. Anmar Afzal, a tenth-grade student, got together with his friends to start a business making face masks to get them through the COVID-19 crisis, which had rendered his father and uncle unemployed. 'I saw surgical masks were in great demand, and people were buying three masks for ₹21. My friends and I managed to get raw materials and make it at home, we decided to sell it for ₹1.' His first order came from his school, which purchased 1,000 masks.

This large-scale experiment has proven beyond doubt that the entrepreneurial mindset can be taught even in the grittiest of environments with great success.[36] We know that not every young person will become an entrepreneur, but we are confident that these youngsters will be far more successful in life because of their entrepreneurial mindset.

Meta-Skill 3: Soft Skills

Google is one of the most data-obsessed companies in the world, so when they set out to try and understand what makes the most effective managers and the highest-performing teams tick, it attracted great interest. In the first study, 'Project Oxygen', Google decided to test its hiring hypothesis by crunching every bit of hiring, firing and promotion data accumulated since the company's incorporation in 1998. The results surprised a lot of people by concluding that, among the most important qualities of Google's top employees, technical skills such as science, technology, engineering and mathematics expertise came in dead last. The top seven characteristics of success at Google are all soft skills:

i.   Being a good coach.
ii. Communicating and listening well.
iii. Including others' different values and points of view.

---

[36]Entrepreneurship Mindset Curriculum (EMC), https://docs.google.com/document/d/12pb6klBNyMsJsd8_0PeSNpJIuttmYUgZ_UuZQ6FLbE4/edit?usp=sharing. Accessed on 24 November 2021.

iv. Having empathy towards and being supportive of colleagues.

v. Being a good critical thinker and problem-solver.

vi. Being able to make connections across complex ideas.[37]

This is validated by a recent poll by the World Economic Forum[38] which asked companies what skills they think are most important and how these are changing. Communication, coordinating with others, the ability to relate (emotional intelligence), managing teams, negotiation or persuasion and working with others to solve complex problems are amongst the most valued of the soft skills. They are seen as more crucial than the so-called hard technical skills, especially if you want to lead larger teams or solve really hard problems.

The 10 Skills	
in 2020	in 2015
1. Complex Problem-Solving	1. Complex Problem-Solving
2. Critical Thinking	2. Coordinating with Others
3. Creativity	3. People Management
4. People Management	4. Critical Thinking
5. Coordinating with Others	5. Negotiation
6. Emotional Intelligence	6. Quality control
7. Judgment and Decision-Making	7. Service Orientation

---

[37]'The surprising thing Google learned about its employees', *The Washington Post*, 20 December 2017, https://www.washingtonpost.com/news/answer-sheet/wp/2017/12/20/the-surprising-thing-google-learned-about-its-employees-and-what-it-means-for-todays-students/. Accessed on 2 December 2021.

[38]'The Future of Jobs Report 2020,' October 2020, https://www3.weforum.org/docs/WEF_Future_of_Jobs_2020.pdf. Accessed on 9 December 2021.

The 10 Skills	
in 2020	in 2015
8. Service Orientation	8. Judgment and Decision-Making
9. Negotiation	9. Active Listening
10. Cognitive Flexibility	10. Creativity

Source: Future of Jobs Report, World Economic Forum

There are, of course, job roles that do not require a lot of people interaction and soft skills. Here are some of them:

- Software programmer
- Transcriptionist
- Data entry clerk
- Laboratory technician
- Librarian
- Truck driver
- Accountant

Not coincidentally, these are all jobs that run the greatest risk of being automated.

The so-called soft skills, which are a combination of common sense, people and social skills and a positive attitude, are critical because they enable people to navigate their environment, work well with others and achieve goals. Soft skills is a term coined by the US Army more than 50 years ago, but is suddenly becoming super important and widely talked about. Why?

One of the interesting paradoxes of the rising levels of automation is that people-interactions are becoming more important rather than less important. Work today is increasingly collaborative and focused on solving complex problems in creative ways. This has become dramatically evident during COVID-19 since the fastest growth was posted by companies like Zoom, Google and Microsoft which provide software services that enable people to collaborate remotely.

Work is also more transdisciplinary than before. For instance, Google hires psychologists to help coders design fonts and anthropologists to better understand how their users think and behave. In a rapidly digitizing world, where humans both collaborate and compete with machines, our success lies not in trying to outrun machines at things that they can do better than us but in becoming more uniquely human. A hundred years from now, there will still be lots of people, and the ability to communicate and collaborate with, relate to and lead people will still be critical.

A final reason is that we have to solve more and more complex problems. Problems can be classified as 'technical' or 'adaptive'. Technical problems, while often challenging, can be solved by applying existing know-how and the organization's current problem-solving processes. Diagnosing and repairing a machine is a technical problem. Machine learning algorithms are getting more and more capable of solving different types of technical problems. Adaptive problems are very different. They require individuals across the organization or even beyond to alter their ways and collaborate. As people themselves are the problem, the solution lies with them. Adaptive problems cannot be solved with expertise or technology alone. More and more of our problems are becoming adaptive. Climate change is the mother of all adaptive problems. So too is the digital transformation of a company, which requires a shift in mindsets, skills and how people work together. The crisis that Boeing had with the 737 Max is another adaptive problem. So is eliminating the use of single-use plastics.

None of these problems can be solved without extraordinary people skills. Even as we automate, the game becomes more and more about people. So, we better learn to get better at our people skills which, at a minimum, includes communication, collaboration, negotiation and working through differences. The ultimate people skill is leadership, which is the ability to get people to rally and work together to achieve something important. This is such a critical issue that I am devoting the entire next chapter to it.

GETTING PRACTICAL

To succeed in the twenty-first century, it is no longer enough to be literate, numerate and graduate with technical or vocational skills. These are but hygiene factors and table stakes. Learning agility, an entrepreneurial mindset and the ability to work well with people and lead them are what will really matter. And the good news is that everyone can learn these and get better at their job. The problem is that these are not taught in school or college or even in a company's training programmes. These skills are hard to learn in a classroom or online. These can only be learnt experientially. So let me conclude with a few ideas for what you can do to strengthen your skills in these areas:

1. Within your organization, take on a big and completely different challenge and make a success of it. The whole point is that the challenge should radically get you out

of your comfort zone and become a 'crucible experience' in which you develop a new mindset and new skills. So, move to a new function or another country, ask for a rural posting, help build a new business for the company or help fix some chronic problem.

2. Volunteer and help solve an important problem in your neighbourhood or community. How do we care for senior citizens living alone during a pandemic? How can we deal with waste? This requires learning to lead by influence, working with people whose views may be very different from yours, interfacing with the government and civil society and finding creative solutions—all of which are extremely valuable. There is no better way to develop your leadership skills than by volunteering.

3. Start a business or, if that is too scary a thought, work as an apprentice in a small neighbourhood business and help it grow (the dhobi, chaiwallah or vegetable vendor, for instance). Or volunteer at a start-up and see if you can add real value and if you like the start-up life.

4. Take a gap year or break and do something completely different. Nipun Mehta of ServiceSpace left home to journey across India on foot along with his wife. Living on a dollar (or less than ₹100) a day, eating whatever food is offered and sleeping wherever a flat surface is found, their journey became a life-changing spiritual pilgrimage. Nipun says, 'As we walked, we learnt much about India, a lot about humanity and most about the stranger we call "I".'

5. Take a course in a subject you have not studied but are interested in and get to a good level of proficiency in it.

6. Teach.

7. Volunteer with a political party and staple yourself to an interesting political leader. Go work in her constituency and participate in an election campaign.

8. Go live in a very different place or country for at least a few months. If you are a student, go live with a relative somewhere or go backpacking across the world on a shoestring budget.

9. Try to become good friends with three people who are different from you. The difference could be in terms of age, gender, religion, interests, nationality or ideology. The bigger the difference, the better.

10. You get the picture.

I started this chapter by saying four meta-skills really matter. I have described three of them: learning agility, entrepreneurial mindset and people skills. What about the fourth? It is leadership. It is the super skill of the twenty-first century, and so critical that I am devoting the entire next chapter to this.

KEY IDEAS

1. For most of the twentieth century, education, particularly higher education, was the ticket to success. This is no longer the case. What matters is having relevant skills to keep up with the times. But what skills should you acquire in a world where software is replacing humans, new technologies are being invented every day, new kinds of jobs and roles are springing into existence and the once hot skills are

quickly becoming irrelevant or commoditized?

2. Your focus must be less on specific skills, such as coding, and more on 'meta-skills'. Meta-skills are higher-order, general skills that enable you to develop new skills. Four meta-skills may be particularly important, namely learning agility, entrepreneurship, soft skills and leadership. These are not skills that can be acquired online or in a classroom; they can only be learnt experientially and particularly through transformative or crucible experiences. The key to acquiring meta-skills is to step outside your comfort zone, take on new and big challenges and see them through.

QUESTION FOR REFLECTION

In the coming year, what are some of the new things that you want to try?

A sabbatical/gap year to do *research business*

Volunteer with *research organization*

A big new professional challenge *improve leadership*

Take a course on *French*

Learn a new skill *creative writing*

Be more adventurous by *making new friends*

'Be the Change': What Leadership in the Twenty-First Century Means

*'I will summarize my view of the world in three simple statements.
Things are better than ever before. Things are still quite bad.
Things can get much worse. This adds up to a somewhat optimistic
view because we are not stuck in the same miserable position for
all of history. There are things we can do to improve the situation.
But there is nothing inevitable about it. It depends on us.'*
—Yuval Noah Harari

༄

Rehan Shaikh is a 12-year-old seventh-grader from a Teach
For India school, who lives in Ahmedabad's Bombay Hotel
area, which is next to the city's main garbage dump. As the
dump grows, it is engulfing the slum where Rehan lives. With
smouldering fires, no water or sanitation and a dreadful stench,
it is a scene from Hell. However, Rehan refused to be crushed
by his environment. Working with his teachers, he started an
organization called Pencilbricks, which is setting up tiny learning
centres where he and his friends teach the younger children in

their community. Nearly 100 children now attend 10 such centres and Rehan and his friends hope to open 100 more, so that no child is left behind. With his confidence boosted by this early success, Rehan started writing letters to the government asking it to address the garbage problem and has tenaciously held it accountable for the promises it has made. When COVID-19 hit, Rehan started looking for ways to ease people's struggles. Here is what he says: 'When I saw people struggling to get food, I felt really bad and wanted to do something. So, I contacted an NGO [non-governmental organization] called Panah Foundation and started taking part in food-distribution efforts with them. We distributed food and grocery kits to 70 families in our first attempt and 120 families in our second.'[39]

When you meet or listen to Rehan, there is no doubt that he is a leader in the true sense of the word. I want to share two more stories of leaders.

Padmashree, my neighbour in Koramangala, Bengaluru, is a homemaker and part-time teacher. Koramangala, like the rest of Bengaluru, has a failing solid waste management system, so there are mounds of garbage in many places. Padmashree was tired of complaining fruitlessly to the municipal authorities, so one day in 2013, she decided enough was enough and started clearing the garbage on her street by herself; a few residents joined her. She then mobilized more residents, including me, as volunteers to clear 'black spots' and beautify them so people would not throw garbage in the same place again. This success then led to a door-to-door campaign to get every house to

---

[39]'Student Leader-Rehan', Vimeo, https://vimeo.com/356868885, Accessed on 22 November 2021.

segregate wet and dry waste and start composting wet waste.
Padmashree then petitioned the local Member of the Legislative
Assembly (MLA) to enforce the ban on single-use plastics
and took on every restaurant and commercial establishment in
our neighbourhood that would not comply. Emboldened by
this success, Padmashree then helped organize a citizens' waste
management task force to work with the municipal authorities
to streamline systems for waste collection and management and
to hold the garbage contractors accountable for their job. The
task force has led major innovations.

Working with a social enterprise called Carbon Masters,
they installed a biogas plant that can convert five tonnes of
wet waste a day into biogas that is used by a local restaurant.
Another unit processes two tonnes per day of leaf litter into
valuable compost. This is in addition to 100 small, standalone leaf
composters across the neighbourhood. A single, two-acre waste-
management centre processes about a ton of waste mattresses
and thermocol every day. A pickup service ensures the proper
disposal of e-waste. Systematic segregation of waste in our
vegetable market now feeds people, cows and pigs, diverting
30 tonnes away from landfills every month. Koramangala
today is a real lighthouse in Bengaluru when it comes to the
management of solid waste and of how citizens, government and
local businesses can work together to solve a tough problem.
Padmashree is now a recognized leader in the space of waste
management whose opinion is sought by companies, legislators
and civic authorities.[40]

---

[40]'Wet waste turned into fuel for restaurant kitchen', *The Hindu*, 4 February 2019,
https://www.thehindu.com/news/cities/bangalore/wet-waste-turned-into-fuel-
for-restaurant-kitchen/article26172159.ece. Accessed on 22 November 2021.

My final story is about Shweta Mukesh, one of my young mentees. After finishing college, Shweta moved back to India from California and started to volunteer with some NGOs engaged in the field of education even as she was working with a tech company. She noticed that the children were hardly taught anything beyond basic mathematics and English. That is when she got the idea of helping young children from the poorest backgrounds to learn about computers and how to code. She started a programme called KidsWhoKode.[41] In just two years, KidsWhoKode developed an effective pedagogy and content and trained over 35,000 children, who learnt to develop video games, websites and mobile applications. The real innovation is that KidsWhoKode is a zero-funds organization. They neither raise funds nor do they charge anything for teaching. Everything is done by volunteers, many of whom are young employees of the many technology companies in Bengaluru. As a result, KidsWhoKode could scale rapidly and now works with partners in 22 states, engaging nearly 200,000 youngsters.[42]

What can we learn about leadership from Rehan, Padmashree and Shweta?

Padmashree, Rehan and Shweta, and thousands of others like them in every part of the world, in organizations, in government and society, illustrate several important ideas about the kind of leadership we need right now. Leadership is simply

---

[41]'Our Programs', <KidsWhoKode/>, https://www.kidswhokode.org/programs. Accessed on 22 November 2021.

[42]Barkha Kumari, 'KidsWhoKode aims to be a student-driven movement: Code of small things', *Bangalore Mirror*, 9 April 2018, https://bangaloremirror.indiatimes.com/bangalore/cover-story/kidswhokode-aims-to-be-a-student-driven-movement-code-of-small-things/articleshow/63672465.cms. Accessed on 22 November 2021.

an act of inspiring a group of people to rally together around a common cause and achieve something essential, something that would not have happened otherwise, something that we could not have individually accomplished.

The most important thing to remember is that leadership is not a title or a position or only about power. Leadership is fundamentally an act. It is about ordinary people doing extraordinary things and becoming extraordinary in that act. Real leaders don't wait for a mandate. They see an opportunity to make a difference and answer an inner call to action. They do not always have formal authority or power; they lead by influence. Nobody asked Rehan or Padmashree to do what they do nor gave them any mandate or authority. This is true within companies and other organizations as well. Just because somebody has the title of 'vice president', does not make them a leader. Many people in such roles are risk-averse bureaucrats whose core strength is organizational politics. They do not have followers, only subordinates. The real leaders in organizations are those who can rally people to make things happen, get things done. Since leadership is a behaviour rather than a position, anyone can be a leader! It is an incredibly important and empowering idea.

Second, leaders are made, not born. There has been this old debate about whether nature or nurture plays a bigger role in a leader. While some people are born with leadership traits, the vast majority of leaders are primarily made by life experiences, or what we call crucible experiences. A crucible experience is when you have to deal with a challenge or environment that is completely outside your experience or comfort zone. It could be the loss of a parent when young, forcing you to become a responsible adult overnight. It could be dealing with some professional crisis. Rising to deal with this challenge transforms how you see the world and yourself and builds new capabilities.

My leadership journey has been a specific set of crucible experiences. When I was young, I was an introvert, lacking self-confidence and most comfortable with books. There was no evidence of leadership ability. Going to study at the Indian Institute of Technology (IIT) Bombay, living for five years in a hostel with 300 rough boys and having to compete academically with some of the smartest people I have ever met was a crucible experience. It taught me social skills and helped develop the ability to relate with a very diverse group of people. It also taught me humility. Going to the US, working and learning to succeed in a tough factory environment, and experiencing racism for the first time was another crucible experience. I developed empathy, tenacity and self-confidence and also learnt to lead by influence. Turning around a failing company called Tata Cummins and helping to make it a successful business was yet another transformational experience where I matured as a business leader and learnt to deal with conflict and adversity with courage. I could go on and on but the point is that becoming a leader is often an intentional journey, and taking on tough challenges which become crucible experiences is a huge part of that journey.

Third, leadership is dependent on context. Think about one of the many traffic jams in an Indian city such as Bengaluru. Someone does something crazy, others get aggressive and soon everything is snarled up and traffic stops. Tempers rise and everyone honks. Invariably some anonymous person steps up and calmly starts directing the traffic. Soon it starts moving again. Our unknown hero disappears. He is a leader at that moment. It is the same with me. I am a leader of some organization, I act as a leader in some situation. The rest of the time I am just another person, often a follower. No one is a 'leader' all the time. A highly effective leader in one context can be a liability in another. Nowhere is this more obvious than in entrepreneurship where a brilliant founder may not be the right person to lead the organization through its growth phase. A highly effective leader in a fluid, entrepreneurial situation may be a miserable failure in a more bureaucratic, rule-based context. Churchill was an enormously effective wartime leader but a miserable failure as a leader of post-war (and pre-war) Britain. Horses for courses.

Also, history's judgment of a leader's contribution or accomplishment will change. Jack Welch, General Electric's CEO for two decades, was celebrated in his time; today, we are less enthusiastic about his ideas and impact. The same is true of so many others like Alan Greenspan of the US Federal Reserve or a political leader such as Margaret Thatcher or Indira Gandhi. We need to remind ourselves of the situation, the context in which they operated and not confuse it with the present moment.

Finally, leaders come in all forms. Leadership styles vary enormously, and leadership effectiveness should *never* be confused with charisma. John Gardner, who was an astute chronicler of leadership, points out how leaders come in many forms, personalities and styles.[43] Some are quiet, some loud.

---

[43]John W. Gardner, *On Leadership*, Free Press, 1993.

Some lead through eloquence, others through their wisdom or courage. It is instructive to look at some historical figures. Churchill was eloquent, Gandhi a visionary who mobilized people by personal example. Vladimir Lenin was coldly purposeful. All three were phenomenal leaders. George Marshall was a self-effacing military leader with superb judgment, while George Patton and Douglas MacArthur were brilliant and flamboyant combat commanders. Dwight Eisenhower was an outstanding administrator and coalition builder who kept the allied forces together. Field Marshal Bernard Montgomery was gifted, temperamental and often insufferable. All were great military leaders in the Second World War but diverse in their personalities.

What you should remember is this—leadership is a mindset and an act, not a title or position. Leaders come in a staggeringly diverse set of personalities and styles, most crucially, anyone can be a leader.

WHY LEADERSHIP MATTERS SO MUCH RIGHT NOW

Leadership is *the* central issue of our time. Rarely in human history has the gap between our challenges and opportunities on one hand and leadership capacity on the other been greater. The gap is evident everywhere—within the organizations where we work, in the communities and cities where we live, our countries and, of course, the world. I don't have to explain this gap—each one of us experiences this yawning chasm every day.

Why do we not have better leadership? The question is asked over and over—in every part of the world, in every

organization and at every level. Ask any CEO what constrains
growth—the answer will not be a lack of opportunities or
resources but a lack of leadership talent that can convert these
opportunities. Ask the Board the same question—you will get
the same answer—only this time it includes the CEO. Why
is a country like India with 1.3 billion people so starved for
more empathetic, more accountable and less corrupt political
leaders? Why can't we do better? Of course, every country
asks the same question. Why are so many vital institutions all
over the world such unaccountable bureaucracies?

Why, like the proverbial boiling frogs, do we see these
problems but not respond vigorously? Why are we collectively
sleepwalking through this period of extreme crisis? Why are
so many of us who are capable of taking a step so anxious
and immobilized?

The reason is simple. We have been conditioned from
childhood to wait for someone with authority and a formal
mandate to come and fix things and rescue us. This delusion
persists into adulthood. So, we wait to be rescued—like the
frogs—while the water gets uncomfortably hot. We wait for
the president of the US—the most powerful country in the
world—to lead the charge on climate change or stop the
conflicts in the Middle East. We wait for the prime minister
to fix an impossible number of things. We wait for our
organization to get a better leader who will empower us
to change things that everyone knows are broken. And, of
course, none of this happens. It cannot and will not happen
because, as Einstein said, rarely are problems fixed by the same
people and thinking that created them. For the people with
power, authority or wealth, the current system has worked

quite well; there is little incentive to try and change things.

It is time to wake up and recognize that the world is not going to improve because of the Big People. Hope is not a strategy either. If things do change for the better, it will be because thousands, then millions of people such as you and I all over the world begin to show leadership. It will change because *you* decide to be a leader. This is what Gandhi meant when he said, 'You must be the change that you wish to see in the world.' The writer Charles Handy adds, 'We cannot wait for great visions from great people, for they are in short supply. It is up to us to light our own small fires in the darkness.'

Solving the many problems that we have requires a different approach. Engineers and scientists can tackle tough computational problems by breaking them down into pieces and then chaining together tens of thousands of processors to solve the pieces. This is a good analogy. To solve the enormous number of problems that we face locally and globally, we need to increase the number of problem-solvers and change leaders by a factor of a thousand or more. We have to get millions of more people believing that they can be leaders, that they can make things better for themselves and others, that they can be the change. We need millions of Rehans and Shwetas. If we are to create better outcomes, leadership has to come from everywhere, not just from people with wealth, power or influence. It has to come from each of us. This is what Bill Drayton, the founder of Ashoka, meant when he said, 'Imagine a world where every person is a change-maker. There is no way then that a problem can outrun a solution.'

THE DEFINING SKILL FOR SUCCESS IN THE
TWENTY-FIRST CENTURY

Precisely because leadership is the central issue for every organization and the world, and because leaders are so scarce, it is *the* defining skill for success in the twenty-first century. Forget about coding, big data, AI or anything else. If you have the ability to get people to rally behind you and tackle challenges, solve problems, go after opportunities, accomplish big goals and you can do this without any formal power, position or mandate, you don't have to worry about opportunities or a job. You are going to flourish. Why? Because most problems and most opportunities (two sides of the same coin really) are complex rather than technical. They require people to work together in teams, across organizations and often across sectors. Take even a relatively straightforward problem such as solid waste management that Padmashree is tackling. The local government alone cannot solve it, nor can businesses. Nor can civil society organizations. Unless all of them come together to try and fix it, there is no progress. This requires a very high order of leadership. The same thing is true within organizations. Every company is trying to become digital. Technologies are a commodity. The real challenge is helping people change their mindset, develop new skills and work differently. It is a challenge of change leadership; if you are good at this, you are golden.

So, developing your leadership skills is extraordinarily important and worthwhile. One of the best ways to learn leadership skills is by volunteering with civic organizations or NGOs because they work on tough problems that require you to work across sectors and inspire followership amongst other volunteers who do not have to listen to you.

And repeating myself one more time—anyone can lead. Everybody can be a leader. It is an act, not a position!

HOW TO BE A LEADER

1. Simply get going

Take the first step, no matter how small it is. A journey of a thousand miles starts with a single step.

The biggest barrier is in our minds. Taking small steps and tackling small problems is a good way to start. In my work with the United Nations Children's Fund (UNICEF), we work with young people from disadvantaged socio-economic backgrounds. We do not talk about leadership. We get them to identify some vexing problem that is bothering them and to do something about it. For instance, the toilet in the school may be broken for a long time and no one is responding to complaints. They are encouraged to find a couple of friends and go fix it. When they succeed, it is like a bulb went off in their head. They are no longer victims. They do not always have to depend on others to fix problems. They are capable of solving some of their own issues! Others were also bothered by the same things and were just waiting for someone to take the lead. Their self-confidence and skills grow. They are ready to take on bigger challenges. They are on their way to becoming leaders.

Leadership is all about action. Successful people have a bias for action. It is possible to spend months or years thinking about how to solve some problem. Or you can choose to jump into the field and start working, trying many things, dumping what doesn't work and embracing the things that do. Get going and figure it out experientially. Rehan didn't have a business plan for his learning centre. He simply experimented with the first one on a shoestring budget and once successful, built the next 10. In the field of entrepreneurship, this approach is called the lean start-up. When in doubt, act boldly as if it is impossible to fail.

2. Become good at sense-making and storytelling

We, humans, are moved by stories more than facts and logic. In our fast-changing world, we need something solid to hold on to, we are often searching for a story or narrative that helps make sense of what is happening around us. So, if you are going to persuade others to join you in your mission, you have to have a knack for sense-making and story-telling. People are overwhelmed with information, frustrated, anxious and unsettled. In this situation, the ability to help people make sense of things, tell the difference between what is important and what is not, and combine all the bits of information into a coherent, simple, hopeful story, a map of the future world, is powerful. This is what creates followers.

'Narrative *is* leadership,' says filmmaker Randy Olson. And the narrative must give hope because leaders are dealers in hope. Authoritarian leaders all over the world understand this and have a simple but appealing story, 'Our country was once great. It no longer is. "They" are the reason for this. If you elect me, I will deal decisively with "them" and make us great again.' Leaders of successful social movements have a visceral understanding of this; think about the simple and powerful statement Black Lives Matter or the Me Too movement, which encouraged women to break their silence and empower each other through empathy and solidarity. Sense-making and storytelling require empathy—the ability to sense and feel the underlying emotions, the assumptions of your future followers.

I did not have the benefit of all this understanding when I became the CEO of Microsoft India. However, after talking to many people, what I sensed was a company that, whilst globally successful, was disliked and distrusted for its lack of empathy and its aggressive business practices. This had resulted in a dangerous alienation of the government and businesses which were all diligently working to explore viable alternatives to Microsoft software. Meanwhile, our modest business in India was also growing at an anaemic rate, a 'Hindu rate of growth'. We came up with a strategy which we called 'Realizing Potential with India'. The core idea was a shift to a mindset of helping people, businesses and the government build useful applications with our software, not simply selling licences and collecting a 'tax'. Every part of the company, every employee was encouraged to think about how Microsoft could contribute meaningfully to India's development. This unleashed a wellspring of creativity which I have described in my book *Conquering the Chaos*.[44] Some of the more noteworthy outcomes were Shiksha, by far the world's largest digital literacy programme; new and more affordable products, such as Windows Starter Edition and a differential pricing system where people were charged based on their ability to pay. Microsoft Research has played a vital role in strengthening India's academic and research capability

---

[44]Ravi Venkatesan, *Conquering the Chaos,* Harvard Business School Press India Limited, 2013.

in computer science. Over the next seven years, our business grew rapidly, Microsoft became the most admired foreign company in India, the pride of our employees in working for the company soared and Microsoft displaced the old favourite Infosys as the best company to work for in India. It all began with a new narrative that said, 'Only if we help Indians and Indian businesses succeed can we succeed.' Narrative is powerful. Believing is seeing.

3. Develop courage

It is impossible to lead if you do not have courage. The leadership journey is completely intertwined with acts of courage. You need courage to get going, to take that first step because there is a risk of being ridiculed or of failing. You need courage to ask for forgiveness rather than permission to do what needs to be done. You need courage to deal with the many setbacks and disappointments along the way. You need courage to stick with your definition of purpose and success even as the world applauds other things. You need courage to speak truth to power, to constructively challenge those with authority and power. You need courage to handle the criticism and scepticism along the way. You need courage to stare down people who question your mandate.

The important thing to remember is that courage is not the absence of fear. It is the ability to function despite your fears. A mentor of mine reminded me that obstacles and fear are what you see when you are not focused on your goal or purpose. The good news is that courage is like any muscle; the more you use it, the stronger it becomes. So, start with small acts of courage.

4. Earn and retain trust

Trust is the primary currency of leadership. If you are going to succeed as a leader, you have to learn to earn the trust of people—both stakeholders and potential 'followers'. This is particularly true when you are leading with influence and have little formal authority. Nobody has to follow you, everybody is a volunteer. How do you earn trust?

The first is a complete and intense commitment to the mission or objective. People must sense and believe that it is not about you, it is only about the mission. This is where a lot of leaders fail—at some point, success and adulation go to their head and their identity becomes intertwined with the cause and the cause merely becomes a vehicle for your success. They become arrogant, vain or authoritarian. And this is when disenchantment sets in, and people begin to drift off.

The second is that you need to lead from the front, especially in difficult moments or on difficult issues. So, when a crisis like COVID-19 hits, as a leader you need to be visible and emotionally connected with people and hands-on in trying to solve problems.

Third, you need to be open-minded and willing to listen. When you have your mind made up and stop listening, you start losing followership. Being open and willing to listen also means a willingness to change your mind, to admit when you are wrong or have made a mistake.

Finally, when sacrifice is called for, the leader must sacrifice first and most before asking others to give up something. Wartime generals know this—they are the last to eat after all the soldiers have been fed. If the organization has to take a pay cut to survive, the CEO needs to be willing to take the deepest cut and do it first.

This is how you earn trust.

5. Understanding power and influence

When you are leading by influence with little or no formal authority, you need to have a keen, instinctive understanding of the dynamics of power and influence. To be effective and successful, you have to change things and quite often against entrenched interests. This is only possible if those who have the power and authority to change things are also willing to support or follow you.

I have had to practise this many times in my career most notably when the Government of India appointed me as non-executive chairman to lead the turnaround of a public-sector bank. When I was being wooed for this, I was promised the freedom, support and formal power to make some of the necessary changes. But I got a big shock when I received my formal appointment letter. It said little about the decision-making powers that were vested in the chair but went into great detail about all the powers that the chairman did *not* have and all the decisions that they were *not* allowed to make. I could not appoint anyone to the board; neither the CEO nor executive management. Neither the board nor its chairman could set the performance targets or decide the compensation for the CEO and management. There are several routine decisions taken by the CEO or the board in a private-sector company which were taken here by the Ministry of Finance. Yet, I was expected to shepherd the turnaround. This was a huge test of leading by influence. Fortunately, working for years in large, bureaucratic, centralized and matrixed companies had given me some good practice. I started by developing a nuanced map of all our stakeholders. Who are the people in the Ministry of Finance and the Reserve Bank of India (RBI) who have the power to make the decisions that we need to make? How do I get them to trust me and support the difficult decisions that we need to make? Who are the people who don't have the authority to make these decisions but influence those who do? Who are the people who do not have the authority to make decisions but can slow things down? (Usually these were board members or senior management.) I spent much of my time developing a relationship of trust and respect with all these people to get them to support important decisions. Creating such a positive spirit and environment allowed the CEO and management to accomplish an extraordinary amount of change that no one believed would be possible. This period is remembered positively by the ministry, the RBI and the employees.

Since leaving the bank, I have been actively involved in several ambitious ventures. I do not have any formal power or authority in any of them, but I do have reasonable influence in most of these situations. I think this is going to be increasingly the norm. More and more of us will have to lead others by influence. One reason is that more of our problems are complex and so require working with a wide cross-section of people from within our organization, across organizations and frequently across sectors (government, business and civil society). This necessarily means learning to work with diverse people with sometimes even divergent interests and where they most certainly do not have to follow you or even listen to you. So, this becomes a crucial skill.

BE THE CHANGE

Former US President Barack Obama says, 'Change will not come if we wait for some other person or some other time. We are the ones we've been waiting for. We are the change that we seek.' This is so true. Our institutions, companies and the world around us will not change for the better just because they need to or because we hope they will. The many problems that bother us will not be solved by others. They will change only if each of us, and enough of us, start leading the change. Fortunately, nearly everyone can lead and this may be our greatest hope.

However, leadership is not just a moral imperative. It is, as I have said, the most useful and important skill if you want to succeed. Moreover, within every one of us is a profound desire to express ourselves, make a difference and feel that our life mattered. Responding to that desire manifests as leadership. Leadership is not some elite calling. It is the unrealized potential in nearly every person.

KEY IDEAS

1. Leadership is the central issue of our time. Rarely in human history has the gap between our challenges and opportunities on one hand and leadership capacity on the other been greater. The gap is evident everywhere—within the organizations where we work, in the communities and cities where we live, our countries and, of course, the

world. To solve the many problems that we face, we need to stop waiting to be rescued by those with power and mandate to do so. Instead, we need to step up and lead. Leadership in this century has to come from everywhere; everybody must be a change-maker.

2. Fortunately, it is also in our self-interest to step up and lead. Precisely because leadership is the central issue for every organization and the world, and because leaders are so scarce, it is *the* defining skill for success in this century. The ability to lead others and to accomplish things by using influence rather than authority is likely the most useful skill to succeed.

3. Leadership is not a title or position. It is an act. Real leaders do not wait for a mandate; they see an opportunity to make a difference and answer an inner call to action. Change will not come if we wait for some other person or some other time. You must be the change that you wish to see in the world.

QUESTIONS FOR REFLECTION

1. Try to recollect a situation at work or in your community where you successfully stepped up to lead without being expected to, without a mandate or any power. How did you accomplish what you did? How did it make you feel?

2. Now try to identify one issue at work or in the world which bothers you and many others and which you believe can be fixed. What is stopping you from tackling it? What are the first couple of steps you could take?

Your GPS to Navigate a Chaotic World

'All games have morals; and the game of Snakes and Ladders captures, as no other activity can hope to do, the eternal truth that for every ladder you climb, a snake is waiting just around the corner; and for every snake, a ladder will compensate.'
—Salman Rushdie, *Midnight's Children*

cs

Snakes and Ladders was a popular board game when I was a child; it is a game of chance, not skill and so I found it comforting. In 1980, for my first coding project at IIT, I built a simulator for Snakes and Ladders. I still like Snakes and Ladders since it strikes me as a nice metaphor for life. The ladders that propel you up are your strengths and efforts meeting good luck. The snakes are random negative events and also bad decisions, they can set you back greatly. The number of snakes on the board seems to be multiplying lately, so learning how to avoid stepping on one is important.

I am not a herpetologist but there appear to be distinct

varieties of 'snakes'. One is temptation. I have long wondered why, with such unfailing regularity, some otherwise extraordinary person shows stunningly bad judgment and ends up ruining their career and life. In India, over the years we have seen business leaders such as Phaneesh Murthy (Infosys), B. Ramalinga Raju (Satyam), Chanda Kochhar (ICICI), Peter Mukerjea (Star TV), Dr Rajendra Pachauri (Intergovernmental Panel on Climate Change [IPCC]) and many others fall from grace. Globally, Bill Clinton, Bill Cosby, Rajat Gupta, Carlos Ghosn, Harvey Weinstein and so many others have not covered themselves with glory. Usually, it is a story of someone succumbing to greed, lust or power.

While it is easy to get judgmental about these fallen leaders, it is important to remember that they were not idiots. They were talented, extremely successful and self-made individuals. None of them started their career intending to do whatever they did, but somewhere, they lost their way. Human weakness prevailed and overshadowed all their strengths and achievements, and they ended up in disgrace. The question for us is this: 'Why do you think this cannot happen to you or me?' It absolutely could and often does but being less visible, our fall from grace is not so spectacular. Someone gets expelled from school for misbehaviour, or sacked from a job for impropriety or loses their family over an affair. Sometimes, it is even more mundane; our weakness or inability to resist some of the seven deadly biblical sins (pride, greed, lust, envy, gluttony, wrath and sloth) results not in infamy but in us simply fizzling out without achieving our potential. Over the years, I have seen this happen to so many good and talented people.

If temptation is one kind of snake, another is a 'really bad decision', particularly around crucial choices such as, 'What should I study/become?', 'Should I join this company or that?', 'I do not like my manager; should I quit this company?', 'Should I take a risk and start a business?', 'Should I marry this person?' and 'Should I emigrate to another country?'

Decisions like these which are costly to reverse deserve deep thinking and multiple perspectives. A poor choice can set you back, in some cases even destroying a person's life. For instance, over the course of my career, I've made some dumb decisions which I regretted. Turning down an offer from Microsoft in 1992 is one of them. Had I had the benefit of better advice, I might have made a better decision. Years later, the opposite happened. I was being recruited as the CEO of an extremely successful company, but one with a mixed reputation. I was all set to join when two of my closest friends beat sense into me. I shudder to think what might have happened had I not changed course.

The third type of snake has to do with what information we choose to believe. This is hugely consequential at a time of so much disinformation, fake news and deepfake videos often spread by extremely charismatic and deeply flawed leaders. For instance, a lot of otherwise sensible people believe in various conspiracy theories about vaccines. They may buy into a story that these are developed by billionaires to control the world or that vaccines can cause autism or infertility. So, they reject a COVID-19 vaccine. I never cease to be amazed at the people I know who buy into various narratives such as COVID-19 being caused by 5G networks or that Muslim men are waging a 'love jihad' to convert Hindu girls or that Joe Biden rigged and 'stole' the US presidential election. While we may laugh at how ridiculous these specific ideas are, we have all seen good and smart people—relatives, colleagues and friends—buy into all kinds of fake news and narratives and follow and worship dangerous leaders. We would not have such polarized societies if this were not the case. This stuff is quite subtle and pernicious, with enormous consequences both for society and for you, personally. So, learning to filter out the false and the fake is an exceptionally important capability in the twenty-first century.

The fourth kind of snake has to do with ethics and ethical choices. There are some choices where right and wrong are clear. Should I steal this? Whatever you end up doing, there is some part of you that knows that it is wrong. However, there is a very large and growing number of choices that are grey. For instance, how much should you pay your maid or employee? Should you pay them just the legal minimum wage or the prevailing market wage? Or should you pay them a living wage that allows them to live with some dignity and educate their children so they can escape poverty? Take a simple thing such as the milk you drink. Are you aware of how it is produced? How much cruelty is involved in it? Do the dairy farmers make a reasonable living? Would you be willing to pay twice as much for less cruel and sustainably produced milk? Would you turn vegan? Knowing the environmental impact of electronics like your phone, how often do you upgrade or buy more gadgets? Do you have a sense of the extent to which social media platforms such as Facebook have undermined responsible journalism and democracy? Knowing this, do you continue to use them, invest in their shares or work for them because the pay is so good?

In all these, and so many more mundane choices we make every day, we can consciously make the world a tiny bit better or worse. There are real consequences for how we feel about ourselves and I also think that there is a 'broken windows' phenomenon when it comes to morality and ethics. Rectitude in small things strengthen our moral fibre and character, and help us resist big temptations and falsehoods. Broken windows is a theory in criminology that believes that a broken window or other visible signs of disorder or decay—think loitering, graffiti, prostitution or drug use—can send the signal that a neighbourhood is uncared for spawning more violent crimes.

The fifth class of snakes are, of course, the random bad events that we call bad luck. Accidents, health issues, getting laid off, and financial and personal setbacks can all be challenging or even catastrophic. There are probably other sorts of dangers lurking out there but my aim is not to be exhaustive but simply point out that our world is getting more chaotic and murkier and we need to have good tools and strategies to avoid stepping on snakes and mines. So what are some of these?

SIX STRATEGIES FOR WARDING OFF SNAKES

1. Choose who you hang out with

A person is known by the company they keep. Motivational speaker Jim Rohn says, 'You are the average of the five people you spend the most time with.' It may be a modest exaggeration but the people we surround ourselves with are the largest influence on our beliefs, values, behaviour and therefore, our life. So, your family, the kids you hang out with in school, who you choose as your friends and your colleagues at work are all powerful influences who can help bring out the best or the worst in you. I can say from personal experience that my ambition to do well academically was the direct result of my friends in high school and at IIT Bombay. I was an indifferent student until I accidentally fell into a group of my classmates who were passionately interested in science, photography and general knowledge and who excelled in their studies. These days, I attribute much of my increase in joy to my decision to spend time entirely with people whose company I enjoy and who I respect.

It can work the other way too. The life of Tony Hsieh, the extraordinary billionaire CEO of Zappos, spiralled out of control in his final year culminating in his death at 46. Cutting himself off from old friends, he surrounded himself with yes-(wo)men who indulged him and exploited him as he experimented with alcohol, drugs and other excesses until his untimely and tragic death. One iconic CEO I once admired profoundly, spent more and more time post-retirement with a small coterie of really warped sycophants. His subsequent bizarre behaviours caused him to lose all the respect he had earned through a lifetime of accomplishment. In her terrific book about young Indians and their aspirations, author Snigdha Poonam describes how many young Indians are anxious, angry, lost and searching for their identity.[45] I was struck by the story of a young insurance salesman, Sunil, who had fallen in with a group of young men who head out every evening to protect cows. This in practice means threatening and beating

---

[45]Snigdha Poonam, *Dreamers: How Young Indians Are Changing Their World*, Viking, 2018.

up Muslim men who are alleged cow-transporters or butchers. He does this because it gives him what he craves for most—a sense of belonging and respect. It is only a matter of time before he gets into trouble. Or maybe not; he may become a successful politician.

There is scientific evidence that shows that our networks shape our life by determining our beliefs and our opportunities or constraints. Changing your networks and who you spend time with, does change your life.

2. Develop a personal board of directors

I was in my early 30s and quite inexperienced when I became the CEO of a large company, reporting to a board of directors. I was fortunate that it was a good board with excellent individuals and a wise chairman. Their counsel and help at every step were hugely important in the eventual success of the enterprise. Learning from this, in every company or venture that I have led since then, I have taken great pains to assemble a good board with terrific individuals to guide us and this has paid off every single time. Along the way, it struck me that I should replicate this for my personal life as well by creating a personal board—a virtual group of people who you assemble in your mind to help you navigate your career and life. Unlike the board of a company, they don't know they exist as a v-team, they never meet together but what they have in common is that they care about you.

I cannot emphasize enough how invaluable my personal board has been to me. From questions like, 'How do I deal with this sticky situation [with some company or some person]?', 'How do I deal with a criminal tenant who is refusing to vacate our home?' to 'Should I join this board? and 'I am ready for another adventure—do you have any ideas?' every professional decision, every conundrum, every challenge I have been able to face in the last 20 years, has been with the help of this amazing group of people.

My personal board has about 25 people. They range from young to quite old. They live in four continents. Some of them are my closest friends. A few are my mentors. Others are simply people whose perspectives I respect and value. Yet others have valuable networks. They have widely different professions, views and interests; that is the point—it is a very diverse group. I consult different people based on the issue. I listen to and consider their views but often decide to do something quite contrarian after some reasoning.

Start building your personal board now if you don't already have something like it. You can start small with just a couple of friends, a mentor or a wise relative. Make sure you have a couple of people who care about you and will tell you the brutal truth whether you want to hear it or not. The list is dynamic and grows gradually over the years. Don't worry about how to give back and make it valuable to the other person. If there is energy in the relationship when you connect, it will probably work. Try to sustain each relationship through genuine engagement and sharing. Connect with many of them when you don't need anything. Share amazing articles that you think will interest them. Surprise them with a book or something they may like. There is no way I can repay some of the people on my board. All I can do is try to be worthy of their time and then 'pay forward'—make myself available and helpful to the next generation.

3. Be careful about where you get your information from

At the end of the day, we are information-processing units and therefore the adage 'garbage in, garbage out' applies. Unfortunately, these are times of disinformation, fake news, conspiracy theories, trolling and compromised journalism. These are also times when powerful people blatantly lie and get away with it. So, like a lot of people, I find it incredibly hard to figure out what is true and what is not, what is a fact, what is fiction and what is a plain old lie. This is not an accident. It is the result of a deliberate effort on the part of different interest groups to flood us with garbage so we can no longer discern facts and truth from falsehood.

In *The Constitution of Knowledge*, Jonathan Rauch explains how for the past few centuries, knowledge has advanced because a decentralized, global community of institutions, academics and experts has tested claims and propositions for error and culled out blatant untruths such as 'Elvis Presley is still alive'.[46] Today, different groups have a strategy to discredit this network of experts and institutions and instead harness the wisdom of crowds and that too its shrillest members. For instance, this allows former US president Donald Trump to make wild, false assertions and if he has enough followers, then these claims become believable.

What do you do in this situation? Even smart, educated and good people have a hard time discerning facts. I have found these measures helpful:

---

[46]Jonathan Rauch, *The Constitution of Knowledge: A Defense of Truth,* Brookings Institution Press, 2021.

i.   Get off most social media especially Facebook,
      Instagram, Twitter and WhatsApp groups. These are
      addictive, notoriously manipulated and distorted
      sources of information, dominated by the shrillest
      voices and with the mindless forwarding of information.
      Even Eric Schmidt, the former CEO of Google, calls
      social media an 'amplifier for idiots'; of all people,
      he should know. Beyond amplifying extreme views
      and false information, compulsive addiction to social
      media hurts sleep, work, relationships, self-worth and
      parenting. So just unplug.[47]

ii.   Rarely is anything good and worthwhile free. So, pick
      a few good newspapers and magazines to subscribe to.
      Pay for good journalism. Even good outfits have biases
      so I subscribe to both conservative and liberal media
      so I can get multiple perspectives. I subscribe to *The
      Economist, Financial Times, The New York Times* and *The
      Wall Street Journal*. I also get *The Indian Express, The Ken,
      The Hindu* and *Business Standard*. These organizations
      too have their biases, but they seem to make an honest
      effort to find and interpret the truth. A lot of other
      media are compromised propaganda machines, so I don't
      bother watching TV or reading any of the papers. If
      there is some important development, I read about that
      specifically.

---

[47] Georgia Wells, Deepa Seetharaman and Jeff Horwitz, 'Is Facebook Bad for You?
It Is for About 360 Million Users, Company Surveys Suggest', *The Wall Street
Journal*, 5 November 2021, https://www.wsj.com/articles/facebook-bad-for-you-
360-million-users-say-yes-company-documents-facebook-files-11636124681.
Accessed 22 November 2021.

iii. Gradually, find voices or people who seem to be thoughtful and balanced, and listen to their views. Avoid the shrill hucksters. Always, always make up your own mind.

iv. The system of peer review has been responsible for humanity's extraordinary progress over the last few centuries, and is a reliable way of filtering out noise and false assertions. So, do not rely on sound-bites and quick opinions to make up your mind. If a topic or issue is important to you, make the effort to find articles, podcasts, videos and books by well-regarded intellectuals from reputable institutions.

4. Develop critical thinking[48]

Historian Yuval Harari makes a brilliant point when he says that humans are fundamentally a post-truth species. We think fundamentally in stories rather than facts, logic or equations. We have been successful as a species because of our unique ability to both create and believe stories. This allows us to get millions of people to cooperate if they buy into the same story. Religion, nationalism and brand marketing, all rely on simple, emotional narratives repeated over and over. Modern leaders and fake news are nothing compared to religious stories that billions of people believe in over thousands of years. So, the problems of fake news and fake narratives are both far older and far more fundamental than most of us realize. Learning to

---

[48]Warren Berger, 'Want to be a better critical thinker? Here's how to spot false narratives and "weaponized lies"', *Quartz*, 22 February 2017, https://qz.com/915723/want-to-be-a-better-critical-thinker-heres-how-to-spot-false-narratives-and-weaponized-lies/. Accessed on 22 November 2021.

distinguish fact and reality from fiction then, is not trivial—we have to work at it. We have to develop what is called 'critical thinking'.

Critical thinking means not blindly accepting a plausible story or explanation, but evaluating it based on the evidence before deciding whether to accept it or not. We have to overcome multiple challenges to do this. First, we are not taught the art of asking thoughtful, sceptical questions. Second, we are bombarded with information; our overloaded brain then tries to simplify things by using a plausible story as shorthand. Finally, to complicate matters, the algorithms at Facebook and other platforms are designed to feed us information that confirms our pre-existing biases. So how do you go about developing critical thinking?

Step one is to recognize that all of us have biases, implicit assumptions and beliefs. You have to start by asking yourself, 'What do I think I know and how do I know it is true?' This requires the humility to accept that you may not know something or might even have it wrong. Then ask yourself: What is the evidence supporting this claim? How reliable is the evidence? Does it come from a trusted source? Is there an agenda behind it? What are they *not* telling me? Finally, critically ask yourself: what is the other side or the other perspective on this issue and is that worth considering?

To use a recent example, let us say you want to find out just how many people died in India due to COVID-19. You can start with the official number of the government which by 27 August 2021, was about 4,36,365 and simply choose to believe it. But then a modest application of mind sows a seed of doubt because somehow this does not seem to fit with the large number of deaths of known people, the anecdotal horror stories of people dying in parking lots of hospitals or for want of oxygen, and the media images of packed crematoria, funeral pyres and bodies floating in the Ganges. So, perhaps the number is higher.

Several Indian and foreign experts and publications have tried to come up with better estimates. One set of estimates converges to a figure of about six to 10 times the official number or between 1.8 and 2.4 million. But even these are questionable because they are extrapolated from unreliable local government data, company records and obituary notices. Other experts have tried to project the number from large sample surveys. These come up with mortality rates that are similar to those in America and would then suggest the number is close to 2.5 million. More recently, a well-regarded data scientist was able to access fairly reliable and official government data (Civil Registration System and Sample Registration System) on the actual number of deaths in two large states. She was then able to calculate the number of 'excess deaths' by month compared to previous, normal years. It is possible to then extrapolate the number of excess deaths, most likely attributable to COVID-19, across other states. This yields an estimate of about 4.4 million. Again, this is an estimate that is based on good data but still has some assumptions. It is now up to you to decide which methodology seems most robust to you and therefore which figure you would believe.

I have used this example to make the point that unless you apply critical thinking, you can get suckered. If you are lazy or gullible, you will likely be manipulated. So, you must be willing to be sceptical and do some work to get multiple less-biased media and expert estimates to get at something approaching the truth. And this is important because the truth you buy into shapes critical assumptions about the competence and integrity of people for instance. Now you cannot do this much work for everything but it is critical to apply such a conscious questioning approach to examine any controversial and divisive claims such as that refugees and immigrants are taking away jobs. The statements of powerful leaders and influential people bear particular scrutiny.

One excellent resource for identifying logical fallacies is Carl Sagan's Baloney Detection Kit.[49] Sagan presents a list of 20 tricks that critical thinkers should always watch out for, including ad hominem attacks (when people ignore the issue at hand and instead attack the character of their opponent), arguments that rely on authority (e.g., 'trust me because I'm the president'), false dichotomies ('you're with us or against us') and 'slippery slope' arguments that suggest one decision will inevitably lead to another grave event.

Another practical resource comes from Adam Grant, who points out that we are frequently in one of three modes—preacher, prosecutor or politician.[50] In preacher mode, we are focused on promoting our own ideas instead of listening. When we are in prosecution mode, we actively attack the ideas of others to win an argument. In politician mode, we are busy

---

[49]Maria Popova, 'The Baloney Detection Kit: Carl Sagan's Rules for Bullshit-Busting and Critical Thinking', *The Marginlian*, https://www.themarginalian. org/2014/01/03/baloney-detection-kit-carl-sagan/. Accessed on 22 November 2021.

[50]Adam Grant, *Think Again: The Power of Knowing What You Don't Know*, Viking, 2021.

seeking the approval of others and have little conviction for
the truth. In each of these modes, the truth takes a back seat,
and being right, defending your beliefs and currying favour
take precedence. Grant's solution is an idea he calls 'rethinking'.
Rethinking is similar to critical thinking, which is an intentional
process of doubting what you know, being curious about what
you don't know and updating your thinking based on new
evidence.

Nobel Prize-winning psychologist Daniel Kahneman
categorized critical thinking as a form of 'slow thinking'; it
requires more effort, time and practise.[51] Most of us would
rather go with our instinctive gut belief (System 1), which seeks
a simple, coherent story above all else and leads us to jump to
conclusions. System 1 does not care too much about the evidence
on which the story is based. Developing our System 2 or slow-
thinking skills not only helps us not fall for false narratives but
also leads to better life decisions. It is an extraordinary book
worth reading carefully.

5. Strengthen your character

Character comprises all the attributes that describe what sort of
a person you are. Do people see you as kind or cruel, honest
or crooked, responsible or irresponsible, generous or mean,
well-mannered or crude, brave or cowardly, fair or ruthless, and
so on? Are you the kind of person who will always take the
easy path or the kind who will strive to do the right thing
even if there is a steep personal cost to this? Our character is

---

[51]Daniel Kahneman, *Thinking, Fast and Slow*, Farrar, Straus and Giroux, 1st
edition (2013).

our internal moral compass—our ability to judge right versus wrong and, most critically, it provides the 'guard rails' that temper our behaviour and prevent our worst excesses. This is precisely why character is so important in a practical sense, not just a moral sense.

We live in a turbulent world, filled with temptations and charlatans, where the truth is murky, and right and wrong are sometimes hard to differentiate.

Moreover, while we may like to believe that dishonesty or bad behaviour will be punished, the unpleasant fact is that a lot of people—including very successful ones—get away with everything, from stealing, lying, cheating and promiscuity to violence, with apparent impunity. With so many of us feeling confused, anxious and craving success, it is so easy to trip up. And everything is okay as long as you get away with it until one day it is not okay. But then your whole world comes crashing down with devastating consequences. This is what happened to each of the famous and successful people I mentioned earlier. And this is why our character becomes so critical. It provides us with a True North to help us apply good judgment to our choices and decisions.

Contrary to popular belief, we achieve our potential and become great not just by focusing on our strengths but also by making sure that our character weaknesses don't undermine us. The inability to control or manage weaknesses is what has prevented a number of talented people from reaching their extraordinary potential or even come crashing to earth. The brutal fact is that at some point in life, we each become the biggest obstacle to our success and whether we can overcome that or not has much to do with character. 'What got you here, won't get you there,' writes the famous executive coach, Marshall Goldsmith.[52]

One of my mentors once gave me memorably tough feedback instead of empathy. The biggest obstacle to your progress is not your manager, your mom, your spouse or the planets and stars. It is you. 'You have to learn to get out of your way,' he said. This is true for all of us. As the saying goes, 'I have seen the enemy, and it is us.' He left me with a thought exercise that I have found to be useful. Imagine you are this giant helium balloon. You have so much lift; you could rise to 50,000 or even 60,000 feet. But here you are, hovering barely off the ground. That is because you are tethered by ropes that are holding you down. This becomes a metaphor for our lives. The balloon represents your enormous potential, the strengths that we each have. The ropes represent the weaknesses that are holding us back. To soar to your potential, you have to systematically untie the ropes and release the balloon. We achieve success by focusing and exploiting our strengths. We avoid failure by confronting our weaknesses.

So, the thought exercise is this: what are the biggest ropes that are holding you down?

What are the repetitive patterns in your behaviour that get you into trouble? Ask your most honest friends or colleagues if you are unsure. Can you untie just one big rope this year? Ask yourself:

i.   What are you most ashamed of? Is there any part of your life that would be embarrassing or worse if it

---

[52]Marshall Goldsmith, *What Got You Here Won't Get You There: How Successful People Become Even More Successful*, Hachette Books, 2007.

were public? Can you put this completely behind you?

ii.   Do you have at least a couple of people in your life who will hold a mirror up to your face or give you the swift kick you need sometimes?

I have many such ropes. But in my late 30s, I had one that was particularly threatening to become a problem. Without realizing it, I was dangerously at risk of becoming a narcissistic CEO. I was driven, addicted to the recognition that comes with success and loved the feeling of power and followership. This in itself is not a problem; a certain amount of narcissism is common amongst leaders and is a big part of their drive for achievement. But the problem is when your need for personal success, fame and power leads you to drive your people and organization too hard. When you are so blinded by your brilliance, you stop listening to others and surround yourself with yes-men and yes-women. It is a precursor to failure. Fortunately, someone held the mirror up to my face in time. Another extremely talented CEO I worked closely with was not so lucky. In his case, he lost the faith of his team and board, who perceived him as both selfish and dangerously out of touch with reality. He was fired.

Strengthening one's character is a lifelong journey towards becoming an increasingly better version of yourself. It is about becoming more self-aware, and making small, daily improvements and more intentional choices that, over time, add up to a huge difference. It results in a more capable internal guidance system that allows you to make better decisions in confusing times and steer clear of snakes, mines and other dangers.

6. Improve your luck through gratitude and by paying forward

I believe that luck matters greatly. There is a tendency amongst successful people to believe they got there largely by their talent, effort and tenacity but there is strong evidence that suggests that luck plays a far greater role than we ever realized. For instance, half of the income differences across people globally is simply explained by where they were born or live. So are differences in life expectancy. And that is just the beginning. Why is one person struck by some catastrophic illness? Why does another win the jackpot by being hired early by a unicorn? One writer has pointed out that you are just one person in a game with seven billion other people and infinite moving parts;[53] the accidental impact of actions outside of your control can be more consequential than the ones you consciously take. I agree with him, though that does not mean we give up or stop trying. It simply means being aware and humble enough to understand that there are many forces and random events that shape the way our life eventually turns out. So, you do your best in every situation and hope for the best.

I know I have been ridiculously lucky so far in my life and I have two daily practices which ensure that the good luck keeps flowing.

The first is the practice of gratitude meditation. For over a decade now, I have trained myself to focus my very first, half-awake thoughts in the morning to enumerate a list of things I am grateful for. I start by giving thanks to the simplest

---

[53]Morgan Housel, *The Psychology of Money: Timeless Lessons on Wealth, Greed, and Happiness*, Harriman House, 2020.

things, such as: that I am alive today, that I am well. That there is abundance in my life, an abundance of love, and an abundance of material comfort. I am blessed with good health, my wife and many good friends. So many people look after us. So many opportunities. I try to count at least 15 things. Then I start on an even more critical list giving thanks to all the really bad things that could happen but have not. There are so many health issues that could affect me but have not. So many kinds of accidents that routinely happen but have not happened in my case. Gratitude for the fact that we are safe and we have not been visited by violence. Gratitude that loved ones are healthy and safe. And so on. It is so easy to take for granted the random bad things that do not happen to us. This meditation practice slowly creates a heightened feeling of gratitude to the Universe, an understanding that we are blessed with grace which I am quite sure, acts as a protective shield. Of course, this is just a belief but I am pretty sure it works!

My second favourite practice to keep good fortune flowing is by paying forward. This is an expression that is used when we don't repay a good deed or kindness to the benefactor but pass it on to others. An example is, when you buy a cup of coffee for a stranger or pay the toll for the car behind you, or make a donation so that the next person taking the meditation course does not have to pay the bill. The reality is that we exist because we stand on the shoulders of millions, if not billions, of others. We owe the food we eat to countless farmers, insects that pollinate, plants, trees and animals. So, how do you repay all this kindness? You pay it forward.

Some years ago, a friend told me the story of Sol Linowitz, one of America's most extraordinary diplomats who negotiated the difficult Panama Canal treaty and was the chairman of Xerox back when it was the Google of its time. When asked about the secret of his incredible success, he responded by saying, 'The truth is; I don't know if what I'm doing is making a difference... [But] Every day I try to do things... Two [kind] things. I may know of someone who is ill, so I'll send some flowers and write a note. Or I may know someone who has just lost a loved one, so I'll write something meaningful and look for a quote that I may have that may bring them some comfort.'[54] I was inspired by this quote and have tried to make it a practice or daily habit. I have found that it is just about being aware of the needs of others and being kind. It is often about really small things such as praising someone who is not expecting it, buying a stranger a cup of tea, feeding a hungry, stray dog, giving a quick meal to a package delivery person who has not had time to stop and eat, being willing to listen to someone who just wants to be heard. Occasionally, it is about going out of the way to help someone in need.

These things help me feel better about myself and I believe that it plays a big role in keeping good fortune flowing in my life. We attract the experiences that we need to grow as human beings, and that is especially true for tough experiences. By cultivating gratitude, kindness and generosity, we reduce the need to be taught a tough lesson in humility.

---

[54]'Sol M. Linowitz,, Congressional Record (Bound Edition), Volume 151 (2005), Part 9 [Senate] [Pages 12850-12854], U.S. Government Publishing Office', https://www.govinfo.gov/content/pkg/CRECB-2005-pt9/html/CRECB-2005-pt9-Pg12850.htm. Accessed on 5 December 2021.

KEY IDEAS

Life in our VUCA world sometimes feels like a game of Snakes and Ladders. Our ladders are effort and talent meeting good luck, and our snakes are bad decisions, poor choices and negative events. An inability to resist temptations as well as taking poor decisions, worshiping false heroes, falling for wrong information and sometimes just plain bad luck can set back our life massively. You need a good internal GPS to navigate this chaos. These six strategies can be helpful:

1. Be choosy about who you hang out with.
2. Develop a personal board of directors.
3. Be careful where you get your information from.
4. Develop critical thinking and don't believe anything blindly.
5. Strengthen you character.
6. Be grateful and pay forward the good luck you have enjoyed.

QUESTIONS FOR REFLECTION

Do the balloon exercise I have described in the chapter.

1. How have your negative character traits sabotaged your success? What can you do to rid yourself of these snakes?
2. Who are the people in your life who fill you with positive energy? Who are the sources of negative energy? Can you change the amount of time you spend with each group?
3. Do you have a few people who could become part of your personal board of directors? How can you best leverage them?

4. How much time do you spend on social media? Does this fill you with positive or negative energy?

5. Where do you primarily get your information from? Who are the people or leaders whose views influence you the most? Apply critical thinking to decide which of them you would continue to rely on.

6. Make your gratitude list and remind yourself of the top three things you are grateful for.

7. What acts of kindness or giving can you develop into a practice?

.6.

How Much Is Enough?

'Money buys happiness in the same way drugs bring pleasure: Incredible if done right, dangerous if used to mask a weakness and disastrous when no amount is enough.'
—Morgan Housel

∽

There is a wonderful short story by Leo Tolstoy called 'How Much Land Does a Man Need?' In the story, a peasant named Pahom is tempted by the Devil into a deal where, for a thousand roubles, he can get as much land as he can cover from sunrise to sunset. Pahom is delighted but gets greedy and pushes himself beyond his endurance. He covers a huge territory and reaches the starting point at sunset but drops dead from exhaustion. He is buried in an ordinary grave only six-feet long, thus answering the question posed by Tolstoy.

The question, 'How much money is enough?' is a central one because we live in a capitalist society where everything comes at a price and money has become a proxy for success. This becomes particularly apparent during a crisis like the

COVID-19 pandemic, where money helped secure access to life-saving oxygen, privileged access to an intensive care unit (ICU) bed or some essential drug. Money is like salt, essential to life but having too much or too little leads to problems. Having the right amount of money is important but having the right attitude towards it is even more so. 'How much is enough?' is a central question that each of us must come to terms with. It is one that I have struggled with.

I was born in a middle-class home in 1960's India, when nobody had much. We were lucky because we had the basics whilst most Indians did not. But I have clear memories of money being tight. Sometimes, it would be a challenge to pay my school fees and there was certainly no surplus for eating out or buying nice things like the stereo or bicycle that I so craved. This made me utterly determined to study hard and land a good job so I could afford such things. Life was kind and by the time I was 25, I was earning more than enough for my modest needs. I have not had to worry about money since. My childhood had left its scars because I remained insecure about money and stayed frugal even amid abundance.

As I have grown older, my income and savings have grown faster than my expenses, which is as it should be, but unfortunately so did my insecurity. I see many people I know struggling to make ends meet.

Since social-safety nets in most countries outside western Europe or Japan are non-existent, people who are struggling to make ends meet live precarious lives, filled with anxiety, sacrifice and little dignity. It is a horrible life. I am not talking about migrant workers; I am talking about out-of-work professionals, unsuccessful entrepreneurs, retired government officers and college professors. They are people just like us. We are living longer and inflation erodes the value of money and savings. Some catastrophic events can blow up your nest egg and such events will be more frequent. Just one health emergency or accident can be devastating. And there are few safety nets. So, I am determined to do my best to not end up like this.

On the other hand, there is greed. Money has come to occupy centre stage in society, wealth has come to denote not just one possible measure of success but the primary metric of it and the media stokes our insecurity and greed. As a result, many professionals who earn a few crores of rupees or 'only' a million dollars feel impoverished compared to others who earn tens or hundreds of millions a year. From time to time, I find that I am not immune to this feeling. When a newspaper publishes CEO salaries, I wonder if I should have stayed on the treadmill longer. Greed and insecurity can be a lethal combination. The philosopher Arthur Schopenhauer accurately observed that money is like seawater; the more we drink, the thirstier we become. It is extraordinarily easy to slip into a mode of chasing more money, and gradually sacrificing more and more of ourselves and our lives to accumulate more wealth. Instead of offering freedom, money then enslaves you and lures you off your path.

One story that made an impression on me is about the famous author Joseph Heller. At a party thrown by a billionaire in New York, another famous author Kurt Vonnegut snidely remarks to Heller that their host, a hedge fund manager, had made more money in a single day than Heller had earned from his wildly popular novel *Catch-22* over its whole history. Heller responds, 'Yes, but I have something he will never have...

the knowledge that I have got *enough*.' The word 'enough' struck a chord with me. I realized that I wanted to get to the same point of security, contentment and abundance. But in an uncertain, unforgiving, mercenary world, how much is enough really? How do I walk that fine balance between falling off the rope versus being enslaved by money? I began an intentional effort to do this and found that it requires not just a mental shift but also several practical actions. I would like to share six ideas that I found really helpful.

1. Money is correlated with happiness but only up to a point

I find that it is very easy to start believing that more money will buy more security and more happiness. This is because it is completely accurate when you have very little money. So, a bit more money buys basic physiological needs of food, shelter and healthcare. A little more allows investment in the future particularly the education of your children. A little more and you can start having some fun. A little more buys security. But then, after a certain point, this correlation begins to break down. That threshold in the developed world is about $75–100,000 per year.[55] In India, given purchasing power parity, the number is probably a monthly income of ₹1 lakh in large cities and half that in smaller towns.

I find it easier to change my mind when there is good data and fortunately there is robust data that supports the hypothesis that money does not buy happiness beyond a

[55]Belinda Luscombe, 'Do We Need $75,000 a Year to Be Happy?' *TIME*, 6 September 2010, http://content.time.com/time/magazine/article/0,9171,2019628,00.html. Accessed on 5 December 2021.

point. In the US, even as life has become more comfortable, happiness has declined. According to the United States Census Bureau, average household income in the US, adjusted for inflation, was higher in 2019 than has ever been recorded for every income quintile. And although income inequality has risen, this has not been mirrored by inequality in the consumption of goods and services. For example, from 2008 to 2019, households in the lowest income quintile increased spending on eating out by an average of about 22 per cent after correcting for inflation; the top quintile increased spending on eating out by an average of just under 8 per cent. New American homes in 2016 were 1,000 square feet larger than in 1973 and living space per person, on an average, has nearly doubled. The number of Americans who use the Internet increased from 52 per cent in 2000 to 90 per cent in 2019. The percentage of those who use social media grew from 5 per cent in 2005 to 72 per cent in 2019. But amid these advances in the quality of life across the income scale, average happiness is decreasing in the US. 'The General Social Survey, which has been measuring social trends among Americans every one or two years since 1972, shows a long-term, gradual decline in happiness—and rise in unhappiness—from 1988 to the present.'[56]

As the ancient philosopher Epicurus said, 'Everything we need to be happy is easy to obtain.' So, the questions to ask yourself if you are beyond this threshold are: 'Why do you want

---

[56] Arthur C. Brooks, 'Are We Trading Our Happiness for Modern Comforts?' *The Atlantic*, 22 October 2020, https://www.theatlantic.com/family/archive/2020/10/why-life-has-gotten-more-comfortable-less-happy/616807/. Accessed on 5 December 2021.

more money? What does money *really* mean to you? Is it a metric of success? Is it an antidote to your insecurity? Does it buy freedom? What does more money buy that you really need?'

I concluded that, for me, it is all of the above but mostly, I value money because it gives me freedom. I am paranoid about being poor. Money simply enables me to do the things that I most care about. But this is a solvable problem with a clear problem statement—'What are the numbers that I need to hit in terms of savings rate and annualized return and risk so that I have a high assurance that I won't become poor?' This is fundamentally a problem of financial planning which brings us to the next point.

2. 'What's your number?'—basic financial planning

A powerful way of defusing anxiety about money is sound financial planning. Financial planning is about taking stock of your current financial situation, your current needs to support the basic lifestyle you wish to have, long-term goals, your risk appetite and capacity and then modelling what you need to do to get there. How much income do you need, and how much of it do you need to save? How do you invest this prudently, how do you create a nest egg to take care of a crisis like losing your job or a major illness and so on?

A shocking number of really smart professionals I know don't do this in a disciplined way. In my case, one of my first managers gave me great advice when I was 25. He said, 'Ravi, save as much as you can. Create a "F**k You Fund" so that you can walk away from your job if it does not fit with your values or you get laid off. You need to be able to live for at least a year on your fund. And go see the financial planner in your bank.' Back then I had no idea what a financial planner does but I am ever grateful for this advice! I did not make a whole lot of money in the first half of my career—especially compared to current compensation levels—and I am a fairly passive investor. But the power of saving well and patiently investing in the stock market over three decades has been magical. The markets in India multiplied by 46 times and the US equities markets grew by five times over this period. Some investments, such as the home we own, did even better. Others such as my angel investments in start-ups fared poorly. Overall, I did much better when I was passive and patient; I did badly when I was greedy and active.

3. Ownership versus licence to use

Only when I joined Microsoft did I begin to understand how intellectual property, such as software, is sold. When you buy software, the seller merely grants you the licence to use it with some terms and conditions. You never actually own it. I realized something obvious, but profound. That it is the same with all our wealth and possessions. We cannot take anything with us; death is the great equalizer. Mukesh Ambani and Jeff Bezos are going to go as empty-handed as you and I. There is a saying that you only take to heaven what you give away on earth.

This idea was accentuated during the financial crash of 2008 when I lost a lot of my stock market wealth. Of course, I felt terrible for days but I also had an epiphany. It dawned on me that much of my wealth is notional; most of it is only digits. It is fluid and can slip away as quickly as it came. If only I had given away earlier what I lost, what a difference

I would have made to the lives of so many people. I kicked myself hard but I learnt a valuable lesson that ownership is notional, and whatever I have, I can lose in a heartbeat. I saw that money is not meant for hoarding; money should flow. I am a conduit, not a tank, and my good fortune must flow.

This idea that humans come with nothing, really 'own' nothing and cannot take anything to the next life is powerful. So why do so many of us still have this urge to hoard money and things? How much of the urge comes from insecurity? How much is just greed in a greedy world? If our need to accumulate is driven by greed or insecurity, no amount of money will be enough. You have to deal with these in your mind and you better start dealing with this as you enter the second half of your life.

4. Minimalism—joy in simplicity

I am not particularly materialistic or acquisitive, but over the years, I have collected a lot of things. Things that I bought, gifts, hand-me-downs from my parents…they all add up. The sheer quantity of it hit me particularly hard when we moved into our own home in 2015. As we packed, my habit of hoarding was laid bare in front of me—boxes of clothes that no longer fit but I hoped to get back into someday, books that I hoped to read. Multiple music systems, fountain pens, watches, three microwave ovens of different vintages, two treadmills and an exercycle (all barely used)! Sentimental stuff I could not bear to throw away. It was a stunning amount for just one person and that too a person who thought he was modest and frugal. How and when did this happen? In my case, it was a lethal combination of five factors: being continuously marketed to, the availability of cheap products from China for every imaginable need, friction-free shopping from Amazon and greater disposable income. And, most problematically, lack of self-control.

It was a spiritual experience. I made some attempts to simplify and declutter, but clearly it was not enough. A couple of years later, I was at a meditation retreat. For three days in the middle of the course, I had a powerful experience of suffocation. I felt myself suffocated by material things. I was horrified by the environmental impact of my blind consumerism. I had reached a point in life where I was gagging on materialism. I finally realized that less is more. More material possessions lead to more baggage. There are more things to worry about and take care of—more onerous tasks and less freedom. I returned home determined to simplify life more drastically.

It turns out, lots of people are feeling this way and are becoming part of a movement called minimalism. The COVID-19 pandemic has helped many of us realize what is important and how little we need beyond the basics. Two terrific resources for those keen on going deeper are Marie Kondo's how-to book on the joy of decluttering and the wonderful Netflix documentary on minimalism.[57] There are a few simple and practical ideas and practices that help:

i. Own a few, high-quality things that will provide lasting pleasure, rather than cheap stuff that you regret buying. I

---

[57]Marie Kondo, *The Life-Changing Magic of Tidying Up: The Japanese Art of Decluttering and Organizing*, Ten Speed Press, 2014.
'Minimalism—A Documentary About the Important Things',
https://www.videoproject.com/Minimalism-Documentary.html. Accessed on 22 November 2021.

had a dear friend, a Parsi gentleman who recently passed away, who exemplified this. He would save money to buy just one nice watch, and would wear it for 50 years. He owned three impeccable suits that he wore for over a decade, a nice car that he owned for four decades and a fine stereo that still looked and sounded good even after 30 years. Every summer, he would get six new linen shirts tailored and give away the previous year's shirts and so on. I think this is a fabulous philosophy.

ii. Don't bring into the house things that you do not need or want. This includes gifts, mementoes received for giving a talk somewhere, prizes and trophies. All this should be given away instantaneously to someone, deserving or not! And if you do bring in something, make sure two things leave.

iii. Once a year, look critically at every single thing you own. Does it bring pleasure or joy? No? Then give it away, sell or throw it away immediately.

iv. Delete that Amazon app on your phone or iPad. It is amazing how much you buy impulsively just because you can.

v. Like intermittent fasting, can you go for a week at a stretch without buying anything at all, other than essentials such as food? Can you go a month? Six months?

It is astonishing how little we need, how much money we can save and how much environmental good we can do by becoming minimalist. But most of all, it is amazing how much lighter and freer we feel.

5. Time value of money

In finance, there is this foundational concept of the time value of money. A dollar today is worth more than a dollar next year. A far more important idea is the 'money value of time'. Time is more precious than money or anything else especially as you are growing older. Ask an old or dying person. What would they not trade away for another few months or years? We value most what we have less of. So, when I turned 50, I intentionally decided to shift gears and start optimizing time rather than other things.

I was fortunate at that time to come across a not-so-particularly noteworthy book, *The 4-Hour Workweek*, which turned out to significantly change my life with an idea.[58] Author Timothy Ferriss proposed that if you prioritize and focus, in just four hours a week, many of us can earn the money to lead a reasonable life. The real challenge, he said, is to figure out what you will do with the rest of the week. Four hours a week? Work just two days a month? I was highly sceptical when I read it in 2012, but there was something quite compelling about this radical idea. So, I did my arithmetic—how much money would I like to earn each month to live comfortably? How do I earn this by working just two days every month? What would I need to charge for the services I provide? To my considerable astonishment, Tim's idea turned out to be feasible, and I have sustained this approach over nearly a decade and given this advice to many others.

---

[58]Timothy Ferriss, *The 4-Hour Workweek: Escape 9-5, Live Anywhere, and Join the New Rich*, Harmony, 2009.

Now I am sure the exact formula may not apply to everyone, but the principle does apply. So, don't reject this as naive or impractical. Some of us may need to work two or three weeks a month. But the reality is that if you can offer something that people value, and you are clear about the value you create and you are super focused on this, it should be possible for you to work far fewer hours than you imagine for money. I come across several people who have not read Timothy's book and would not articulate things the same way, but have arranged their lives similarly. So, work for money for a small part of the time and do the things that you find worthwhile and purposeful the rest of the time. Ideally, do what you love and find a way to get paid for it.

The second important idea is to use the money you earn to buy yourself either more time or more convenience. It is a simple idea—pay people to do things. Spend money not on things but on services and experiences. These bring joy, free up time and, in the process, you provide someone with a livelihood too. When I was little, we used to travel by train during our summer vacation. When we reached the railway station, my father would always use a porter. We were not rich and could have easily carried our few bags. But my father insisted on using a porter because it gave someone a livelihood. It also reduced stress since the porter would know exactly where to go, whether the train was on time, how to properly stow away the luggage and so on. It was a huge lesson for a young boy. So, today, I employ many services and people. It frees up time, makes things convenient and supports many families.

6. Abundance, scarcity and poverty

In his 1990 bestseller, *The 7 Habits of Highly Effective People*, author Stephen Covey reintroduced an old concept—the difference between an abundance mindset and a scarcity mindset.[59] The abundance mindset is a paradigm which is grounded in the belief that there is more than enough for everyone. It flows out of a deep inner sense of personal worth, security and faith in the fundamental goodness of the world.

A scarcity mindset is a belief that there will never be enough. It is a mindset that has us thinking there is not enough out there—not enough time, not enough money or love or opportunities or happiness. It is a zero-sum game where one person's gain is another person's loss, so it has us thinking from a position of scarcity. This leads to anxiety, stress and fear. Because we fear losing what we have, we cling to it and try to hoard it and grab a bit more for ourselves. And because we believe things are scarce, we get bogged down with envy and anxiety. There is a lot of 'if-only' feelings where we find ourselves wishing, 'If only I had more money... If only I had more time.'

Nipun Mehta writes extensively about abundance and poverty, particularly, poverty of the heart. He helped me become aware that there are so many forms of capital beyond money; there is time, kindness, love, networks, expertise and reputation. He also helped me understand that you can have all the wealth in the world but if you do not have a large heart, compassion and generosity, you will still feel poor. It is poverty of a different

---

[59]Stephen R. Covey, *The 7 Habits of Highly Effective People: Powerful Lessons in Personal Change*, Simon & Schuster, 2013.

sort—it is the poverty of spirit.

Abundance and scarcity—while the former mindset will set you free, the latter will imprison you. Some people are lucky because their childhood experiences and upbringing instil an abundance mentality and generosity of spirit. Others like me have to consciously cultivate this. But it is eminently possible. I found these practices very helpful:

i.   Cultivate gratitude: Every day, consciously remember all the things that you have to be grateful for, including health, safety, love, friends, money, opportunity and freedom. Use this to change your mind's narrative and start convincing yourself that you are blessed and wealthy. Gradually, the feeling of abundance will start to take root.

ii. Practise generosity: Every time we give instead of take, our fists and hearts gradually unclench. There is much joy in giving and we never miss what we have given away. You start feeling better about yourself. It becomes easier to give a bit more each time. So, make giving a habit and pretty soon the flywheel will gather speed.

iii. Hang out with people who have an abundance mentality: Minimize the time you spend with people who have a scarcity mindset. Both abundance and scarcity are contagious states of mind.

Remember, even if you have a scarcity mindset, it is not permanent. You can change it.

KEY IDEAS

In our capitalist society, money is like salt—essential to life but too much or too little of it can cause difficulties. Having the right amount of money is important but having the right attitude towards it is even more so. 'How much is enough?' is a central question that each of us must come to terms with. The following five ideas, if implemented well, can help a lot:

1. Realize that money brings happiness but only up to a point.
2. Disciplined financial planning and saving are critical.
3. Minimalism is good for the planet, for your overall happiness and savings.
4. For most of us, time is more valuable than money. Therefore, optimize accordingly.
5. You can be rich yet feel poor and vice versa. An abundance mindset is crucial.

IDEAS FOR ACTION

1. Watch a YouTube or Netflix video of Marie Kondo and see if you can radically declutter your possessions.
2. Build a financial plan and model, and explore how much you will need to earn, save and invest to live your ideal life.
3. If possible, plan a 'two-day workweek' for yourself—one that might satisfy your financial needs. How would you use the remainder of your time?

Navigate Your Career: 10 Practical Ideas

'Do the best you can with what you are best at.'
—Charles Handy

∽

In this chapter, I want to share 10 practical ideas that may help you think about your work and career. Over the years, many people have come to me for advice and found these ideas to be very useful.

1. Forget about jobs

Unemployment is a huge issue in most parts of the world with the exception of some hot sector, a few fast-growing economies such as the US or pockets of worker shortages as the world recovers from the pandemic. In most parts of the world—South Asia, Africa and South America—there will be far fewer decent jobs than job seekers and no such thing as job security. This is structural and exacerbated by the pandemic. Employers want ever more flexible labour contracts, so the use of contractors, outsourcing and gig workers will grow. Remote work is here to stay, accelerating these trends.

So, I advise people to aspire, as fast as possible, to become self-employed, a freelancer, a gig worker or, better yet, an entrepreneur. A job is still necessary for most of us to get started professionally, but may be best viewed as a useful launch pad to these pathways rather than a good, long-term goal.

More and more people will need to become self-employed and contract out their talent as services. More of us will choose to work remotely, often from home. As we do, our work life will begin to resemble a series of projects or gigs. At any given moment, work will be a portfolio of projects, some of which will be compensated, while others will provide rewards like meaning/purpose and fun. As some projects end, new ones will start. Sometimes, a project may last several years and at other times, there may be a series of projects, lasting several years, with a single client. But it would be a mistake to start considering the longer projects as stable, long-term jobs. By all means, enjoy the ride while it lasts, but don't frame it as a job with a long career span, unless it is an exceptional organization with a genuine commitment to people.

Many people at first find this to be an overwhelming or even terrifying idea. A common reaction is, 'What! A world without a job for me? There is no way I can do this! I better hold on tightly to my job and hope it lasts till I retire.' It definitely can be scary at first, but there is enormous freedom, a sense of liberation, when you finally figure this out. I know this from personal experience.

When I was contemplating a shift from the industrial economy to the software industry with Microsoft in 2003, I was very conflicted. The opportunity was exciting but it was also scary with a high probability of failure.

Most of my friends, family and mentors thought it was too risky and advised against it. I teetered back and forth. Finally, I asked myself, 'What would I regret more at 50? Passing on the opportunity because I was afraid to fail? Or that I gave it my best shot but that it did not work out?' So, I decided to frame this not as a job with a long career but rather as a project. I saw myself as a sort of project manager. I was fully prepared for the job to be a short project, however, it lasted a good eight years.

I have retained this mindset. I was super clear that I didn't want to be an employee ever again. Since then, my work has been a dynamic bundle or portfolio of projects.

Some of the projects have been compensated, such as board positions. Others give me meaning, joy or an opportunity to learn something new. It is a fun and rich way to live life. I don't have to answer to a manager I don't respect. I don't have to worry about what comes after the job. For the first time, I feel as though I am reasonably in charge of my life and time, instead of someone else. Over the years, I know many people who have successfully made this transition, some voluntarily and others by compulsion. The key is to have some valuable skills that people are willing to pay for, a good network and some self-confidence.

The same thinking applies to the idea of careers as well. We need to think about careers, not as ladders to be climbed, but more as a series of interesting adventures. On the last day of my MBA programme in 1992, there was a session on how to think about work and career. Our professor warned us that there was no longer any job security and that most of us would have to navigate three or four transitions in our career. That turned out to be true for most of us, with some notable exceptions who have made their entire career with a single organization. However, the current and future generations will have to think not about a few transitions but rather how to navigate a maze—and that too a magical Harry Potter maze, where there are unexpected challenges and adventures at every turn. You *must* have this spirit of adventure and the mindset of an explorer if you want to have fun and be successful in the twenty-first century.

2. Join the 'passion economy'

When it comes to work, a person today faces a bewildering set of choices.

It felt easier 20 or 30 years ago, when the world was simpler. If you were ambitious and came from a middle-class family, you had to be an engineer, doctor, scientist, teacher or a civil servant. Today, success can take infinitely more forms. With the rise of an array of new platforms, you can do anything from anywhere if you can find a way to make a living out of it; you can be a maths tutor, stand-up comedian, a writer, bitcoin trader or an entrepreneur. Unfortunately, there is little by way of counselling to help people figure out their path in this thicket of choices. This is what leads to anxiety, confusion and even despair.

The challenge or trick is in finding the convergence or intersection of what you love doing, what you are good at, what the world needs and what you can get paid for. The Japanese have a term for this—'Ikigai' or your reason for living. It is believed to be the key to satisfaction and longevity and it turns out to be a useful way to think about what you should do in a world of many confusing possibilities. Today, this age-old concept is manifesting as what is called 'The Passion Economy', which is an economy driven by people who find a way to build small businesses around what they are good at and what they love doing. In a book by the same name, Adam Davidson shows that there are unprecedented new opportunities to make a living while doing what you love.[60] It is no longer a choice between being rich and miserable doing something you don't like, or being happy but poor.

Adam gives many examples of ordinary people who could see an opportunity for a small business, which is a perfect fit with their talent and interests, right under their nose. He goes on to provide a set of principles of success for these businesses. A good example of a passion entrepreneur whom we work with at GAME, is Sumedha Mahajan, a young woman from Amritsar who runs India's first sportswear brand specifically designed for women. Sumedha is an endurance runner and whilst running a 1,500 kilometre race from Delhi to Mumbai, she experienced first-hand the challenges that women runners faced with their gear. This inspired her to start Brakefree; her mission is to ensure that women don't have to 'adjust' to men's sportswear. Brakefree is on a tear.

Kuldeep Dantewadia is another passion entrepreneur. After getting an MBA in 2009, Kuldeep boarded the Jagriti Yatra, a train journey that carries aspiring and accomplished Indian

---

[60] Adam Davidson, *The Passion Economy: The New Rules for Thriving in the Twenty-First Century*, Knopf, 2020.

innovators across the length and breadth of the country. The experience affirmed his determination to do something about the environment. Driven by enthusiasm, and without much of a plan, Dantewadia, with a few friends, started collecting garbage and spent six months understanding the garbage economy. In 2011, Dantewadia and two of his friends formed Reap Benefit with two key objectives: finding behavioural change models and developing affordable ways towards more sustainable living. They went beyond garbage and looked at water, energy and green habitats. As of 2021, they have successfully engaged 34,000 young leaders who have diverted 665,000 tons of waste from landfills, saved 1.7-megawatt hours of energy and 46 million litres of water. And they are just getting started.

Passion economy may sound similar to gig economy, but to me, it feels fundamentally different. Gig economy seems to put the platform (such as Uber, DoorDash or Swiggy) at the centre and people are simply the necessary hands that perform tasks, for which they are paid some nominal amount. The bulk of the value created is appropriated by the platform owners and customers. In passion economy, the individual is at the centre. The individual sees an opportunity to build a product, service or experience that reflects who they are—what they love, they value and excel at—and find a segment that is willing to pay for it. They leverage platforms as needed but don't serve the platform nor are exploited by it. Andreessen Horowitz, one of the top venture capital firms in the world, sees passion economy as the future of work and gives examples of teachers earning thousands of dollars each month by teaching virtual classes on various platforms, the top-earning writer on the newsletter platform Substack earning more than $500,000 a year from reader subscriptions and the top content creator on Podia, a platform for video courses, making more than $100,000 a month.

I find the idea of passion economy very empowering and optimistic at a time where there is so much gloom and doom about the future of jobs and work. However, if this idea is to take off, it will require lots of catalytic interventions to make it a movement. The idea has to catch on and become more aspirational by showcasing lots of successful passion entrepreneurs. People will need some training to spot opportunities around them and will have to learn the basics of business, know what platforms exist, learn from peers, understand how to access capital and so on. This is the mission at GAME, the organization I founded to create an entrepreneurial movement.

3. Don't chase opportunities. Attract them!

If a mouse enters your house, it is generally a bad idea to try and chase it and hunt it down. The tried-and-tested approach is to set out some tasty bait and attract the animal into a trap. It is the same with jobs and opportunities. What you want to do is make yourself so attractive that opportunities are drawn to you, and not the other way around. Applying for jobs on job sites, chasing headhunters, etc., is a frustrating game of low probabilities and endless heartbreak.

When I look back at my 35-year-long career, I see that that is how it has worked out. I chased innumerable opportunities without much success. And yet, all the best professional experiences came into my life when I did not pursue them. So, when it comes to finding opportunities, think marketing and not sales.

So how do you attract opportunities? Here is what I would advise:

i. Get going. Grab the best opportunity available now that fits with your interest and talent. If nothing is the right fit, but you need to make money, grab it anyway. Remember, nothing is forever and no job is beneath your dignity if it is all you have. Some of the world's most successful people have started from extremely modest beginnings. Dhirubhai Ambani was a gas station attendant in Yemen. Steve Jobs was homeless at one point in his life and ate free food at a Hare Krishna temple. Where you start does not matter, what you *do*, does.

ii. Excel at your work. Do more than what people expect of you. Take initiative and show a can-do, positive attitude. Demonstrate leadership. Get along with your boss no matter what you think of him. Leave a legacy, so you are remembered after you have gone. Build your reputation around excellence, dependability and integrity.

    This idea of leaving a legacy is really important. So many people I know simply live year to year in some job or role, and then move on. Like the ocean quickly wipes away your footprints in the sand, no one remembers either the person or their work. However, even in an entry-level frontline job or in an individual contributor role and certainly, if you are leading a team or function, it is possible to stand out both in terms of your results and in your conduct, in a way that people remember. Like a bright and shining presence.

iii. Stand out of the crowd. In the world of marketing, differentiation is everything. In a world filled with others like you, all of whom are looking to get ahead, how do you stand out? Excelling and leaving a legacy are important but it is also important to be noticed. In the animal world, there is a behaviour called 'stotting'; a gazelle in the grassland, for example, springs up and down in the same place, essentially signalling to watching predators that they are agile and fit, thereby getting them to focus on other, less fit, prey.

So, how do you signal your fitness to your relevant audience? This can be achieved by thoughtfully and intentionally cultivating your reputation. This is not the same as incessant self-promotion, which people can see through and tire of. You build your professional and personal reputation by joining relevant professional organizations (such as the Institute of Electrical and Electronics Engineers [IEEE] and the American Society of Mechanical Engineers [ASME], if you are an engineer), by giving talks about different aspects of your work, by writing on topics that interest you, by showing thought leadership on some of these matters and slowly developing a distinctive voice and some followership. This has worked well for me. I started writing about my work quite early on and enjoyed this. By good luck, one of my pieces got published as an article, 'Cummins Engine Flexes its Factories', in the *Harvard Business Review* as far back as 1990.[61] This helped me get accepted to a good MBA programme and also got the attention of the CEO of the company, Cummins Engine Company, putting me on a different trajectory. I have stayed with this and continue

---

[61] Ravi Venkatesan, 'Cummins Engine Flexes its Factories', *Harvard Business Review*, Issue: March–April 1990, https://hbr.org/1990/03/cummins-engine-flexes-its-factory. Accessed on 19 September 2021.

to write and speak about a variety of issues that interest me. This led to my first book, *Conquering the Chaos*, and now a second. Sheryl Sandberg, chief operating officer (COO) of Facebook, advises young professionals to 'develop your voice, not your brand'[62] and this seems quite sound to me.

4. Catch a big wave

One of the most important criteria that venture investors use to make investment decisions is simply the size of the market or opportunity. A potentially massive market means that there is room both for many successful firms and also enough headroom for at least a few firms to become super big. It is not a bad criterion to use in deciding where to play yourself. A rising tide lifts all boats and a really big wave can catapult even mediocre talent to extraordinary success. A lot of what we take for success is simply the result of our judgment or the luck of being in the right place at the right time.

Looking back at my career, I can think of three big waves. The first was globalization, especially the integration of China and India into the global system. The second wave was the advent of the Internet. And the third was the financialization of the world where value extraction became more important than value creation. It made those who controlled capital into masters of the universe. I participated in and benefitted mightily from the first. I was a relative latecomer to tech and did not stay long enough during the second wave. And I largely skipped the third except as a passive stock market investor. Even just

[62]Theodore Kinni, 'Sheryl Sandberg: Develop Your Voice, Not Your Brand', Standford Business, 17 July 2017, https://www.gsb.stanford.edu/insights/sheryl-sandberg-develop-your-voice-not-your-brand. Accessed on 5 December 2021.

barely putting my toe in the water enabled me to do much better than I had imagined possible when I graduated in 1992. But my success paled in comparison to those who simply either had the luck or smarts to catch one of the big waves and then simply ride it.

Working across multiple industries allowed me to see this starkly. I have worked in three different industries: the industrial economy with firms such as Cummins, Volvo and Hitachi; in tech with Microsoft and Infosys and in financial services with Bank of Baroda and several venture funds. What I realized is that, a mediocre person in a rising industry will do much better than a star talent in a less dynamic industry. I met and worked with some exceptionally smart and worthy people in industrial firms. They led satisfying lives but with modest compensation and modest opportunities for growth. But in comparison, I continue to see quite mediocre people become jaw-droppingly successful and wealthy, both in tech and in financial services, simply because they were lifted by the rising tide of their industry. Nearly 40 years ago, Michael E. Porter, at Harvard Business School, became famous because of his insight that the dynamics of an industry determines the profit potential of a company much more than how well it is run. In other words, a well-run company in a tough industry will make far less money than a mediocrely run firm in an attractive industry. It took me a long time to realize that this applies to talent too.

This has huge implications for you especially if you are south of 40. As we look at this century, where are the next big waves? The Internet economy has yet to peak with still massive opportunities in blockchain, AI, etc. Tackling climate change and decarbonizing the world will require investments, innovation and entrepreneurship and creating wealth that could dwarf the Internet. Then there are big opportunities in synthetic biology and life sciences. There is going to be an embarrassment of riches. But 80 per cent of success is showing up, so pick one of the next big waves early and find a way to participate in it. Again, Sheryl Sandberg nailed it when she said, 'Get on a rocket ship. When companies are growing quickly and they are having a lot of impact, careers take care of themselves. If you are offered a seat on a rocket ship, don't ask what seat. Just get on.'

5. Geography is destiny

The Arab scholar Ibn Khaldun said it first in the fourteenth century 'Geography is destiny.'

He was prophetic. Where you are born and where you live determine your fate, opportunities and constraints and your values and beliefs to a greater extent than almost anything else.

If you are born in a violent, conflict-ridden place such as Afghanistan, El Salvador, Syria or Sudan, or in caste- and race-dominated states like Uttar Pradesh (UP) in India or Mississippi in the American south, it doesn't matter how much talent and drive you have, it is an uphill task to climb up in life and prosper. The gravity is just enormous. Your entire focus must be on just one thing—to get out. You need to get to a place where not only is there more opportunity, you need to get to a place that has embraced modern values.

Most people understand that it is far better to be in a place with lots of opportunities rather than one that is an opportunity desert. But what matters much, much more than opportunity is the dominant societal values of the place where you choose to live and work.

The central importance of a society embracing modern values was taught to me by my mentor Edmund Phelps.[63] Phelps was awarded the Nobel Memorial Prize in economic sciences in 2006 and his work explores why some societies prosper and others don't. His contrarian conclusion is that, it all starts with the beliefs of people. Have they embraced modern values? For instance, there is the belief that everyone has the right to pursue their dreams and make their own decisions. Does society appreciate risk-taking and accept failure in that process? Does it believe that everyone has potential or does one have to be male or from some religion or caste for their ability to be validated? Who are the role models and what are the success archetypes? Is it inventors, entrepreneurs and scientists who create new knowledge and businesses or corrupt and wealthy politicians, police and civil servants? What do people believe about justice and about the enforcement of laws? These are the beliefs that allowed England to march ahead and become the world's most powerful and wealthy nation in the eighteenth and nineteenth centuries. These beliefs led to America becoming dynamic and dominating the world in the twentieth century.

As these ideas sank in, I realized why Silicon Valley is so vibrant and what makes Bengaluru and Mumbai such dynamic, entrepreneurial hubs. It also outlined for me how oppressive places can never flourish. The reality is that there

---

[63]Edmund Phelps, Raicho Bojilov, Hian Teck Hoon and Gylfi Zoega, *Dynamism: The Values That Drive Innovation, Job Satisfaction, and Economic Growth*, Harvard University Press, 2020.

are opportunities everywhere—even in Afghanistan, Yemen, Haiti, Bihar and UP. Societal values determine the nature of the opportunities that are on offer. In some places, the best opportunities for wealth and power are in becoming a warlord, petty criminal, drug lord or arms dealer. In other places, the best opportunities are to invent, tinker, create and build. Places with opportunities and modern values—that's where you want to be!

One of my wise mentors once told me that if he had to live life all over again, he would pick the place or city first, and then figure out what to do. I now think he had it right. It is the reason why I live in Bengaluru. No, it is not the glorious weather or the tech ecosystem. More than any other city in India, Bengaluru has embraced modern, liberal values. It will continue to flourish despite the best efforts of the politicians.

6. How to find your next s-curve

In the good old days of the twentieth century, a career resembled a ladder. If you were an ambitious professional, you found a good job and steadily climbed the ladder till you hit a ceiling and then you waited for retirement. This construct is obsolete.

I think it is now much more helpful to see your professional life as a series of s-curves. The term 's-curve' is used to describe how a new product or technology is adopted, and ultimately replaced by the next new thing.

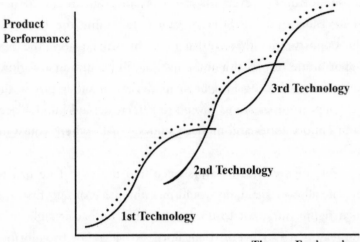

It is a useful way to think about your work life and see how to represent it in this way. For instance, my first s-curve started in 1987, when I first started work as an engineer, eventually growing to a senior management role. I think of my experience at Microsoft as my second s-curve, because it was such a different experience qualitatively and opened the door to so much more. As a freelancer with a portfolio of interests, I am now on my third s-curve. If I live long enough and am lucky, I will be able to reinvent myself yet again and end up on a fourth s-curve.

For my generation, this progression across curves is a bit exceptional. However, I can already see that more and more people are going to make such transitions in this century— either by choice or by compulsion. Think of it as shifting gears in a car—moving to higher and higher gears till you hit your peak potential.

How do you know when it is time to try to make a shift to the next curve? And how do you find your next s-curve?

The signal or impetus that tells you that it is time to shift comes in two ways. Sometimes life gives you a blow; you get laid off, your start-up goes under or some other disaster forces you to start making a change. Or, often, it creeps up unannounced and manifests as boredom, frustration and dissatisfaction. What you do no longer gives you joy and you hate your employers. In fact, it is insufferable. You know that you need to make a change but you don't know what to do next and jobs, even uninspiring ones, are hard to come by. Here ask yourself, as Steve Jobs did, 'If today were the last day of my life, would I want to do what I am about to do today? And whenever the answer has been "No" for too many days in a row, I know I need to change something.'

We all reach a point where we know the things we do not want to do, but are not clear about what we *do* want to do next. Too many people in this situation resign themselves to a life of quiet desperation, holding on to the vine they have and hoping things will improve. Some quit their job only to take up something much like what they had left; this can turn out to be a situation of jumping out of the frying pan into the fire. The reality is that most often this crisis is life's impetus to nudge you to search for your next curve. It calls for an intentional search process.

This is exactly the situation I found myself in back in 2011. I was bored at Microsoft. The building work was done, the goals I had set in 2004 were nearly met and I did not have enthusiasm for the next phase. I knew it was time for change, except I did not know what I wanted to do next. And the many perks of the role made me want to keep holding on.

If you find yourself in a situation like this, you should know that you cannot think your way to your next s-curve. You have to experiment and feel your way to your future. Deng Xiaoping put it beautifully, 'You have to cross the river by feeling your way across the stones.' So, what I did was conduct many experiments and tried my hand at lots of different things. These experiments told me a lot about myself. I learnt about what energized me (solving tough problems) versus what might at best be a hobby (teaching). I understood which paths were open and promising and which doors were firmly closed. Through a process of trial and experimentation—think of it as design thinking applied to your life—I began to gradually discover the shape of my next s-curve.

Many things that I thought might be terrific either did not work out or I realized that it was not for me. For instance, I tried to start a company that would deliver simple cloud-based solutions for small businesses. I got a great team together and built a business plan. We had an angel investor before I realized that I did not have passion for the venture and the journey to make the company a successful enterprise. I was doing it simply because the start-up fever in Bengaluru had got to me. We pulled the plug on it. I then tried to bring a couple of global tech companies to India, not as an employee but as a partner, but that did not work out either. There were other things I did. I ended up joining the boards of interesting companies, such as Volvo, Infosys and Bank of Baroda, as they went through difficult transitions. My first book did really well and got me on the path of writing, speaking and teaching, which I enjoy greatly. I found that I loved to think about how to improve the world around me; this led to fulfilling adventures with Social Venture Partners, Unitus, GAME, the Rockefeller Foundation and UNICEF. Gradually, I have developed what is popularly called a portfolio life—a set of projects that give me purpose, joy and opportunities to learn; a couple of them pay money while most are pro bono. Collectively, they give me all that I need.

I think this approach might work quite well for many people who are unsure and confused about what to do and searching for what might come next. I suggest that you take the Stanford University course called 'Designing Your Life'.[64] Think about things you're good at or would like to do. Teach. Serve. Start a business leading people on cycling adventures. Or as my friend Anshu did, see if you can cut it as a stand-up comedian. Move to a village and live sustainably with nature. Whatever. Try each of these things, build prototypes of the experience and test them to see what works. *Do* you enjoy it? Can you make a living out of it?

The approach is not always easy and I discovered that it can be extremely uncomfortable; it is easy to feel lost, anxious, frustrated or depressed. This is because our work is often inextricably connected to our sense of identity. What we do for a living forms a major part of our life story. The process of changing careers or shifting s-curves is, therefore, often a process of changing identity.[65] Advice such as 'Do what you love and love what you do,' can feel simplistic and naive. The

---

[64]Bill Burnett and Dave Evans, *Designing Your Life*; https://designingyour.life/.
[65]Herminia Ibarra, *Working Identity: Unconventional Strategies for Reinventing Your Career*, Harvard Business Review Press, 2004.

nat the transition can be a difficult journey, a tentative on full of false starts, disappointments and occasional small victories until we reach the other shore.

And there is no guarantee that you will reach the other side or find your next s-curve. But here is the thing to remember—there is the risk that you may fail to find your next thing or flail around much longer before you find it. But the bigger risk is that you stay stuck. I have always found errors of commission to be better than errors of omission. At least there is some sense that you are in charge of your destiny, that you can course-correct. It is better than being a passive victim hoping things will get better. So many terrific people I know have plateaued and are wasting the best years of their life hoping to be rescued. If you want to dig deeper, Deepak Jayaraman, a coach who advises people on transitions, has built a terrific set of resources.[66]

7. Networks really matter

I sometimes get my friends to do an exercise. You might want to try it too. Make two lists. On one list, write down the names of the most important people who have influenced your life. For instance, your parents, spouse, close friends, mentor, manager, etc. On the second, write down the jobs or most meaningful experiences you've had. Now think carefully about how each of these came to be? Did you make it happen? Or did the person or opportunity enter your life?

This can be an eye-opening exercise for a lot of people; it

---

[66]Deepak Jayaraman, 'Play to Potential,' https://www.playtopotential.com. Accessed on 22 November 2021.

was for me when I first did it. That is because we go around with the delusion that we make things happen whereas much more than half of all the opportunities and people simply 'enter' your life. But how exactly does this work? It turns out that they come into your life through your networks. So, as an illustration, here are some of my work experiences and how they happened:

Microsoft: I was introduced by a close friend who works at one of the top executive search firms.

Infosys: I worked closely with the founder when I was at Microsoft; he invited me to the Board.

Bank of Baroda: A classmate was in the finance ministry and when the Bank needed someone dependable, he approached me.

Rockefeller Foundation: I was introduced by a good friend who was a board member.

UNICEF: I met UNICEF Executive Director, Henrietta H. Fore at a conference. We appreciated each other's talks, which led to a discussion on youth, jobs and entrepreneurship. When she became executive director of UNICEF, she approached me to take on this work.

GAME: I met my co-founders at another social enterprise I had started. Most of the team and the CEO came through our networks. The funders—Ikea Foundation, Bill & Melinda Gates Foundation (BMGF), Omidyar Network, Tata Trusts and Rockefeller Foundation—were all people I had worked with.

Every major opportunity came not through my efforts, but through my networks. I met the most important people in my life, including my wife and closest friends, in a similarly serendipitous way. It isn't magic—it's your networks.

So, your networks shape your life to an extraordinary extent. I am lucky because, completely by accident, I have developed good, broad networks that have helped attract extremely diverse people and opportunities. But you can be more intentional about this. In a powerful article, James Currier describes how much of what we take for chance or luck is actually powerfully determined or constrained by our networks.[67] Specifically, he points out that six networks overwhelmingly shape your beliefs and values, and determine which opportunities present themselves. These networks include where you are born and the family you are born into, the high school and college that you attend, your first job, your partner or spouse and the city you live in.

The most effective way to change your life, for better or for worse, is to change who you are surrounded by or who you hang out with. *Change your networks to change your life.* So, if you are interested in entrepreneurship, moving to a hot spot like Silicon Valley, Bengaluru or simply hanging out at places and events where venture capitalists and entrepreneurs congregate is bound to bring entrepreneurial ideas and opportunities. Of course, these days online networks are really important as well.

There are tons of resources on the Internet on how to build your networks; in particular, Herminia Ibarra, an organizational behaviour professor at London Business School, usefully points out the need for three very different types of networks—personal, operational and strategic—and the need to

---

[67]James Currier, 'Your Life is Driven by Network Effects', *NfX*, https://www. nfx.com/post/your-life-network-effects/. Accessed on 19 September 2021.

be intentional about building these networks.[68] A lot of people are uncomfortable with the idea of consciously building their professional networks because it seems unsavoury to get ahead based on who you know, rather than what you know. But in a networked world, networking is an essential and critical skill. Networking is most effective when you are genuinely interested in people and have something of value to offer, especially expertise and help. Otherwise, people will see you for what you are—just another self-promoting schmoozer.

8. Walk your own path

In a famous speech at Stanford University, Steve Jobs gave this advice to students, 'Your time is limited, so don't waste it living someone else's life. Don't be trapped by dogma—which is living with the results of other people's thinking. Don't let the noise of others' opinions drown out your own inner voice. And most important, have the courage to follow your heart and intuition. They somehow already know what you truly want to become. Everything else is secondary.'[69]

This is fantastic advice and hard to say it any better. Steve's words made a huge impact on me. I spent too many years measuring up to and living by other people's definition of success. Fortunately, I realized this in time and have spent the last decade finding my path. Many people realize their folly only much later and have a lot of regret about a life wasted.

---

[68]Herminia Ibarra and Mark Lee Hunter, 'How Leaders Create and Use Networks', *Harvard Business Review*, January 2007, https://hbr.org/2007/01/how-leaders-create-and-use-networks. Accessed on 22 November 2021.
[69]'"You've got to find what you love," Jobs says', Stanford News, 14 June 2005, https://news.stanford.edu/news/2005/june15/jobs-061505.html. Accessed on 22 November 2021.

The fundamental point is that you are unique. There is no one else exactly like you. You are here to figure out the answer to the question, 'Why am I here?' You cannot do that by living someone else's life. You are also most likely to be successful and impactful by discovering your own path rather than by walking someone else's.

The challenge for most of us is shedding years of conditioning or programming and developing the courage to take the road less travelled? How do you then experientially find your way? How do you develop your own definition of success? How do you avoid the many temptations and false trails along the way? For a lot of people, including me, it takes a lot of intentional experiments as I will share in the next chapter

9. Learn to live a portfolio life

I have already shared my belief that many more of us will be self-employed, and our work can be conceptualized as an evolving collection of projects. This portfolio is dynamic and evolves over time as some projects get completed and new ones are added. Such an approach offers us much more flexibility and freedom to shape work into the way we want to live rather than the other way around. As a result, we will have the opportunity to integrate other activities and interests, including family time, having fun, learning and contributing to society much better. This way of operating is often called a portfolio life. It used to be a way some people arranged their life post-retirement, but with people living and needing to remain active much longer, and traditional employment opportunities dwindling, more and more of us will need to build ourselves a portfolio life even sooner.

I have lived a portfolio life ever since I renounced full-time employment, a decade ago, when I was in my mid-40s. Building and living a portfolio life does take significant adjustment. It was difficult, disorienting and uncomfortable for me in the beginning. It was the first time in my life that I didn't have a consuming job, that I didn't have to wake up and immediately head to work. I would be all alone at home while the rest of the world was at work. It was the first time that I didn't have a structured, intense week or any responsibility for other people. This phase of de-addiction from work can cause all kinds of dark thoughts to well up and it is what makes it so tempting to want to quickly go back to a familiar job. But I stayed with it and leaned into my discomfort. This allowed me to understand just how important work is to me, and indeed to all of us.

Work is about much more than just putting food on the table. About a century ago, Abraham Maslow proposed a hierarchy of human needs for psychological well-being. In his hierarchy, once basic physiological and safety needs are met, there is a need for belonging, for accomplishment and for recognition and finally for a sense of purpose. Good work can satisfy many of these needs. Decent work provides an income that permits a life of dignity. Like oxygen, it is essential for life.

Work provides opportunities for expression, achievement, recognition and learning. As President Roosevelt said, 'Happiness lies not in the mere possession of money; it lies in the joy of achievement, in the thrill of creative effort.' It is a source of identity and belonging. We often identify ourselves by either our profession (software developer, poet, founder) or organization. Without such an affiliation, how do you explain who you are?

Work provides community, especially when we work 12 hours a day. Our colleagues are often our closest friends. When you take it away, it is easy to feel adrift or lonely.

Work provides structure to our days without which it is so easy to become lazy and dissolute. After the first few days when it was fun to be unshaven and still in pyjamas at 11:00 am, I began to worry that this would soon lead to drinking early and who knows what else! So, I quickly got myself a small office at a business centre so I could head out there and have some semblance of a routine.

Most important of all, work can provide purpose. If you are a physician and you define your purpose in life as healing people (as opposed to becoming rich), it makes your whole existence worthwhile.

The nice thing about a good job is that it satisfies most of these needs—all you have to do is plug in and play. When you strike out on your own, when you try to construct a portfolio life, you have to solve each of these things yourself. What can you do that people are willing to pay enough for you to meet your financial needs? How will you introduce yourself to strangers? How will you develop a routine and structure for your days? And so on. This requires a fair amount of intentional design-your-life experiments before you converge on what works for you.

There are good resources out there if you want to learn more about how to build your portfolio life. David Corbett's book is still a classic.[70]

---

[70]David D. Corbett and Richard Higgins, *Portfolio Life: The New Path to Work, Purpose, and Passion After 50*; Jossey-Bass, 1st edition, 2006.

10. There is no such thing as retirement

The first person to live to 150 has been born. Many of us, with some luck and care, will live into our 90s. So the idea of retiring at 60 or 65 is woefully out of date. Over the years, by watching relatives and friends age, I have seen that the quality of our ageing is largely determined by our mindset more than our genes or circumstances. Those who no longer have a purpose and cease to be intellectually engaged, and physically and socially active, start deteriorating rapidly. Those who see age as simply a number, find purposeful things to immerse themselves in and stay active, do remarkably well. I have many inspirations in my life. Three friends whom I admire the most—Bob Berg, Frank Wisner and Edmund Phelps—are all in their 80s and are extraordinarily active and engaged in various pursuits. My father-in-law used to teach business policy at a college until quite recently, when his hearing went out; he is 94. A maternal aunt just gave a public dance performance at 82. Another aunt received a PhD at 74. My neighbour Gopal just crushed his opponent to win the seniors' badminton title; he is over 80 years old and his hapless opponent, 60. Joe Biden, the president of the US, is 79. My friend Ashok Soota founded his company Happiest Minds in 2011; he was 70 at the time and had a successful initial public offering (IPO) a decade later. All of them remind us that age is just a number.

As I turn 58, I see the next 20 years (if I do live that long) as simply another s-curve; an opportunity for new adventures. I think I am just approaching peak performance and peak impact and my fear is not that my best is behind me but that I will run out of time to do the things I want to do. I used to have a quote by John Denver pinned above my desk that said, 'Today is the first day of the rest of my life'. It has shaped my belief that everything I have done before, all that I have learnt, all my assets are merely a foundation or launch pad for what I am to do next. I believe that the world really needs what I have to offer and therefore my most useful work and contributions and best years lie ahead of me. The point is not whether this idea is right. It is the belief that matters and belief is often self-fulfilling.

There are plenty of excellent resources on living a full life. Harvard sociologist Sarah Lawrence-Lightfoot talks about a 'Third Chapter'—a middle period between 50 and 75, where we are neither young nor old. She says that in the Third Chapter, we must shift into a different gear to find new ways of exploring and channelling our passions, energies, skills and resources into new areas.[71] Teresa Amabile has a terrific podcast about the challenges posed by retirement, particularly the need to reinvent identity and find a new purpose.[72] Lynda Gratton's book on *The 100-Year Life* also has lots of good advice on how to think about the second half of our life.[73] Bob Buford's book, *Halftime: Moving from Success to Significance* remains a classic.[74]

Ageing is not an easy process. I can see that already. But

[71]Sara Lawrence-Lightfoot, *The Third Chapter: Passion, Risk, and Adventure in the 25 Years After 50*, FSG; First edition (2009)

[72]Prof. Teresa Amabile, 'How Retirement Changes your Identity', *Harvard Business Review*, 15 January 2019, https://hbr.org/podcast/2019/01/how-retirement-changes-your-identity. Accessed on 22 November 2021.

[73]Lynda Gratton and Andrew Scott, *The 100-Year Life: Living and Working in an Age of Longevity*, Bloomsbury Information; Export/Airside edition (2016).

[74]Bob Buford, *Halftime: Moving from Success to Significance*, Zondervan; Anniversary edition (2015).

the twilight years of life may be the most transformative and fulfilling chapter of our lives, where experience, wisdom and altruism come together in a beautiful way

QUESTIONS FOR REFLECTION

1. Find your ikigai. Draw these four intersecting circles and take the time to fill them out. How aligned is what you are doing with your ikigai?

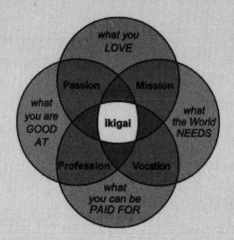

Source: Ikigai-EN.svg, Wikimedia Commons

2. If you are not already self-employed, a freelancer or an entrepreneur, what is it that you would or could do if you were suddenly forced by circumstances to support yourself? What skills do you have that people value and might pay for? How could you convert this into a microbusiness and become a passion entrepreneur?

3. Are you in a good city with a vibrant culture and abundant opportunities? Does living there energize you? Should you

move? Where should you move to? When?

4. What megatrend are you riding?

5. Retrace the trajectory of your life in the shape of one
    or more s-curves. Which part of the s-curve are you on
    presently? Are you learning and accomplishing new things
    at a steep rate or have you plateaued? Are there cues or
    signs that it may be time to make a change? If yes, how
    are you going to find your next s-curve?

.8.

Reflecting on Success and Happiness

*'The plain fact is that the planet does not need more successful
people. But it does desperately need more peacemakers,
healers, restorers, storytellers and lovers. It needs people of moral
courage willing to join the fight to make the world habitable and
humane. And these qualities have little to do
with success as we have defined it.'*
—David Orr

∽

There are defining moments in our life that change the way
we think and who we are. One summer day in June 2011
turned out to be such a defining moment for me. I remember
that day even now. It was a stable and carefree point in my life.
I was on a vacation in the US and had decided to visit my
old boss, who lived on a beautiful ranch close to Yellowstone
National Park. I reached there late in the afternoon and Tim
suggested that it being such a gorgeous day, I should go sit
by the stream that flowed through the ranch. It seemed like a
great idea. So there I was, in one of the most beautiful places,

with not a care or worry, not a cloud in the sky. It was perfect. Except that I could not enjoy myself. My mind was anxious and unsettled, thinking of the past and future, everywhere but the present. I was miserable in paradise. That was when the penny dropped for me. I finally experienced that happiness is a state of mind rather than the result of external circumstances. I had spent many years working hard to achieve reasonable success and to arrange everything in my life to perfection. Had I made a checklist of criteria for being happy, I am pretty sure I would have ticked most of them that day. And yet, when I was in a perfect moment, I was anxious and dissatisfied. Here was clear evidence that I was living in my mind and thoughts rather than in the world around me.

Normally, I would forget such a moment but this time, I held on to it. I could see that there was an important lesson to be learnt and so I leaned into the experience. I was reasonably successful but neither happy nor content. Instead of savouring my success and good luck, I was often disappointed and anxious. I began to see that I had been chasing success because I thought it would make me happy but it no longer brought me joy. As I probed further, I realized that from early childhood, a powerful 'theory of happiness' had been programmed into me. It went like this: work hard. Hard work leads to achievement. Achievement leads to success, which is recognition, promotions and money. Success leads to happiness.

I was programmed and driven to work hard and keep achieving. It dawned on me that achievement and success had little to do with happiness. As I looked around me, I saw plenty of successful people who were unhappy and many happy, content people who had not achieved much in the world's eyes. I was now a full-fledged success addict. This turns out to be a quite common pattern, particularly in high achievers. The late Clay Christensen, professor of business administration at Harvard Business School, observed that many of us are wired with a high need for achievement, and like a drug, we get a pretty big kick every time we achieve something.[75] It could be a bonus or a raise, a promotion, a tweet or a video going viral. It is exhilarating to see ourselves succeed in life. And we keep doing the same things to continue that cycle of success. The problem is that this is not what makes us happy in the long run.

No matter how much you achieve, it gives only momentary pleasure but it is never good enough. You don't feel appreciated enough; you feel like you are not getting the recognition you deserve. So, you redouble your efforts and seek greater heights of achievement. Psychologists have a term for this; it is called the hedonic treadmill.[76] The more you achieve, the more you require to sustain your new levels of satisfaction. Gratification is temporary. It results in a pointless quest for more and more. There is no solution to this except to jump off the treadmill.

So here I was in my late 40s, and my theory of happiness, which had served me well so far and had resulted in many accomplishments and success, was breaking down. It was time to come up with a better theory.

---

[75]Clayton M. Christensen, 'How Will You Measure Your Life?' *Harvard Business Review*, (July–August 2010), https://hbr.org/2010/07/how-will-you-measure-your-life. Accessed on 22 November 2021.

[76]Seph Fontane Pennock, 'The Hedonic Treadmill: Are We Forever Chasing Rainbows?' PositivePsychology.com, 13 September 2021, https://positivepsychology.com/hedonic-treadmill/. Accessed on 22 November 2021.

One of the things you realize as you grow older is that there is nothing unique about you or your journey. You are just one of the billions who have made the same journey through the ages. Every insight or 'aha' that you have is new only to you; it has very likely already been observed and written about for centuries and millennia before. Nearly 100 years ago, the psychoanalyst Carl Jung had said that there are three acts in a person's life. The first is when he sets out to conquer the world. The second act is when he realizes that the world is not likely to be conquered by the likes of him. The final act is coming to peace with this. I realized that I had reached the end of my second act and it was time to make peace by finding a new purpose.

There are many good books on happiness and especially on midlife transition.[77] Most of these books agree on one point: midlife is when you get many signals to start turning inwards and become more intentional about your spiritual development. It is the time to ask what I have called the 'big questions'. Author David Brooks says that life is about climbing two mountains. We graduate from college, start a career and family and begin climbing the mountain we think we are meant to climb. Our goals are what society endorses—to be successful and make a mark. But when we get to the top of the mountain and look around, we find the view unsatisfying. We realize that there is a bigger mountain out there that is

---

[77]David Brooks, *The Second Mountain: The Quest for a Moral Life*, Random House, 2019.

Bob Buford, *Halftime: Moving from Success to Significance*, Zondervan, 2015.

James Hollis, *Finding Meaning in the Second Half of Life: How to Finally, Really Grow Up*, Avery, 2006.

our real goal. And so, we descend and start climbing again but this time, with a difference. This time, the goals are not about us. It is about the people and things we care about, not those that society tells us to value.

In 2011, I descended the first mountain and began climbing my second mountain. It is still very much a work-in-progress. I am not sure that I have even reached base camp but it at least feels like I am on the right mountain this time.

It has been observed that the most important life lessons cannot be taught; they must be experienced. You do not learn the most valuable lessons until you go through your journey. But I think that there is still some value in sharing what I have learnt so that it may affirm your journey. In that spirit, here are some of my most significant learnings about success and happiness.

1. Success is a delusion unless you define it for yourself

When you measure your life by someone else's definition of success, it tends to be subjective, fleeting and relative and, therefore, unsatisfying.

No matter what I had achieved, in every dimension, I could see others who were even more successful. I knew people who were seemingly happier, more sorted and accomplished, richer, more famous or more powerful. As the Jedi knight, Qui-Gon Jin said in *Star Wars I: The Phantom Menace*, 'There's always a bigger fish.'

Success is fleeting as is life itself... You can be seen as a success today and forgotten tomorrow. Think about sports stars, actors, famous CEOs and powerful politicians of just a few years ago. The spotlight moves on. All of us and our achievements are destined to be quickly forgotten and that is just a blunt fact.

Success is subjective because it lies in the mind of the viewer. You may consider someone to be successful; I might have a different view. That is because we may have different metrics for measuring success.

There is also a world of difference between being successful, being seen as successful and feeling successful. These are three quite different things. You can be successful in the eyes of the world but never feel so. Conversely, I have seen people whom the world barely noticed but who *felt* successful and satisfied. I see this in our driver Waheed, who is content and always peaceful, unruffled even when his little boy was diagnosed with leukaemia. I see this even more in Lakshmi, the ever-smiling lady who sells flowers near our home. Despite many challenges, she remains radiant, drawing people to her. So, clearly, you do not have to be successful to feel successful and content. And there are lots of people who are neither successful nor feel successful but try desperately to look successful.

The problem is not success per se but rather falling into the trap of living by other people's definition of success. The challenge is to develop your own authentic definition of success, of how you will measure your life and then live by this. I found that incredibly hard to do. Like many of us, I had been programmed from childhood by parents and teachers to crave affirmation, praise and recognition. As a child, you get scolded or punished when you don't do what they want. You get praised and rewarded when you do. Praise feels good. The withdrawal of love and affirmation feels terrible. Many of us learn to toe the line; some like me get hooked on praise. This continues into adulthood where our manager and then our social networks also play the same game.

Learning not to care what other people think, to no longer care greatly about recognition and praise, and to live according to your definition of success is critical for freedom, for happiness and also for doing anything truly useful. When you look at people with originality—think Gandhi, Einstein, Picasso, Steve Jobs or Elon Musk for instance—you will see that being free and having the courage to walk your own path are critical to doing something path-breaking.

However, all this is easier said than done. The success delusion, the addiction to affirmation is easy to diagnose but harder to wean off than even cocaine. I have been at it for a whole decade and these things still matter but a whole lot less than before. Three things helped me get over it. First, I finally understood that no one cares about what I am up to. They are not thinking about me because they are busy thinking about what others think about them. What also helped greatly is seeing that ultimately, most of us are irrelevant, except to ourselves and a very few others. We, our lives, our achievements, all are destined to be quickly forgotten. So why bother living up to someone else's measure of success? Why not at least find my way now? But these realizations are at an intellectual level, whereas the need for affirmation is often very deep. I found that working with a skilled counsellor or coach can be quite effective. Coaching has helped me see that I am fine as I am, that what matters to people I care about is who I am as a person and how I engage with them, not how successful I am. This is finally enabling me to peel off from the herd and walk my own path. It still sometimes gets lonely and, of course, I still find myself occasionally wanting affirmation and recognition. But such moments are fewer as my newer definition of a life well-lived slowly takes root.

2. To control your happiness, control your mind

In one famous, and to me mind-boggling experiment, a person who has their arm amputated and a person who wins a lottery are both at their prior levels of happiness six months after the event. Building on this, scientists like Dan Gilbert have been able to show that happiness is not correlated with our external circumstances; both happiness and misery are synthesized by your mind and have fairly little to do with your reality.[78] If you are joyous by nature, you are happy regardless of what you have or don't have. The converse is also true. Poets and philosophers have known this for a long time. 'The mind is its own place and, in itself can make a heaven of hell or a hell of heaven,' said John Milton. So, scientists and philosophers both agree that the biggest determinant of happiness and satisfaction is becoming the master of your mind.

Yet, how hard it is to control the mind! Swami Vivekananda has a very good way of describing this. There was a monkey, he said, restless by nature as all monkeys are. As if that were not enough, someone made him drink wine freely so that he became even more restless. Then a scorpion stung the monkey so he found his condition worse than ever. To complete his misery, a demon possessed him. The human mind is like that monkey, hyperactive, then drunk with the wine of desire,

---

[78]Daniel Gilbert, *Stumbling on Happiness*, Vintage, 2007.

thus increasing its turbulence. After desire, comes the sting of the scorpion of jealousy at the success of others. Finally, the demon of pride enters the mind, making it think of itself as all-important. How hard it is to control such a restless mind! But as long as your mind controls you rather than the other way around, you can neither be at peace nor effective. The difference between an ordinary person and a great person is just concentration. The quality of your life depends on your concentration and what you concentrate on, says Swamiji.

Spiritual teacher Eckhart Tolle, who has influenced me deeply, observes that the biggest barrier to happiness, for most people, is identification with the constant chatter of the mind. Many of us are completely in sync with our thoughts and with the continuously chattering voice in our heads. The voice incessantly interprets reality and judges, criticizes and determines our emotional reactions. It leads us to imagine ourselves to be the stream of chatter and believe that we are the voice in our head. This sense of self that we construct from identifying with our thoughts is the source of the ego—the idea that we are a separate being, distinct from everything and everyone else. This ego, according to Tolle, sustains itself through dissatisfaction with the present moment, constantly projecting into the future so that happiness is forever in the future and absent from the present.

No matter what life stage you are at, what your circumstances, you will be happier and more effective if you learn to tame your mind and dissociate yourself from your thoughts. For me, this is the ultimate challenge. My monkey mind is never quiet; it chatters and jumps about endlessly. Dark and negative thoughts well up for no good reason. My mind is rarely in the present and prefers to dwell on the past with regret or on the future with anxiety. It takes for granted all the good things in my life—people, health, love, resources, respect—and hankers after what I do not have. It rebels when I think of exercise and just loves all sorts of unhealthy things. Years of multitasking and smartphone addiction have made it even more fidgety, affecting my ability to focus and concentrate.

So, I know that I have to tame my wilful monkey and have been at it for some years. There are many books and videos with useful techniques but in my experience, the one really effective path is that of any serious meditation practice such as vipassana. S.N. Goenka, the foremost teacher of vipassana, describes the goal as equanimity, a state in which the mind stays calm, does not react to thoughts, and therefore has no great cravings or aversions and is not unduly affected by the ups and downs of life.

It is really hard to sustain the practice of meditation day after day. After several years of uneven daily practice, I find myself making slow progress—two steps forward and one step back. Now, at last, I can separate myself from my thoughts and see them as passing clouds generated by my mind. But they still have immense power over me, and I have so many miles to go yet. Taming my monkey mind is at the top of my bucket list.

3. Find your purpose and define your commitments

Having a sense of purpose is critical to feeling good about yourself and your life. It gives meaning to your life and concentrates your mind and energies towards a positive outcome. Mark Twain put it wonderfully when he wrote,

'The two most important days in your life are the day you are born and the day you find out why.'

The vast majority of people are on an existential treadmill, where the bulk of their waking hours and energy is consumed by simply meeting their basic needs. They neither have the time to think about purpose nor to read this book. Amongst people like us, a few find the purpose of their life quite early on and easily. Many artists, writers and scientists are like this. I was fortunate because, for most of the first half of my life, I had a clear sense of purpose—it was simply to excel, succeed and see how far I could get up my 'first mountain'. But after climbing down the first mountain, I had to find my 'second mountain'.

I realized that you cannot sit in your room and think your way to your purpose. There is no way other than to feel your way experientially to it. It can take a lifetime. I drew inspiration from Gandhi, who was the ultimate design thinker. Over five decades, he intentionally conducted innumerable experiments—varying his diet and his dress sense, deciding to go to England and then moving to South Africa before returning to India, developing an intimate understanding of his country, reading Tolstoy, Thoreau, the Bhagavad Gita and Bible and testing and refining his ideas—to arrive at a clearer sense of himself, the world and how to effect change in it.[79]

Inspired by Gandhi's approach, I have conducted my own experiments to find my path. Ignoring the monkey law ('never let go of a vine without having a firm grip on another'), I

---

[79]Mahatma Gandhi, *The Story of My Experiments with Truth*, Fingerprint Publishing, 2009.

walked away from a rewarding job without much of a plan. Some of the experiments were in the realm of work. I joined the boards of interesting companies and tried my hand as a social entrepreneur and investor. I wrote my first book and began to write, speak and teach more often. I began to declutter my life, choosing to retain the relationships, things and activities that gave me joy. And then there were the experiments to find an approach to spirituality that felt right to me. These included lots of reading and YouTube videos, encounters with self-declared gurus and different meditation methods.

What I concluded is that statements of purpose, while directionally helpful, can be too abstract for practical purposes. For instance, here are some real examples of purpose:

'To positively impact the lives of every person I meet.'

'To find the highest value use of me.'

'To become a better and better version of myself.'

You can see the issue. They sound good but are too abstract, can sound a bit preachy and can apply to any person. You need a way to bring these down to a practical level. For this, I found it more useful to think in terms of my commitments. I am particularly grateful to my friend and colleague, Russ Eisenstat for this. He maddeningly kept pushing me to articulate my commitments. 'You are your commitments', Russ kept drilling into my head. 'What is it that anchors you? What are the things that really matter to you? What are you in service of?' Russ kept insisting. He helped me see five categories of commitments:

i.   Commitment to your spouse and family: How do you support them in achieving their aspirations? How do you become a real unit? How do you merge your identity?

ii. Commitment to your vocation: We each have a talent and some assets. How do we nurture these and put this to serve others?

iii. Commitment to your faith: How to develop a philosophy of life and live it?

iv. Commitment to your community: How do we nurture meaningful relationships? How do you serve your community?

v. Commitment to yourself: How to make time for the things that you enjoy? How do you create the discipline of continuous improvement?

It sounds easy but it is not. I found it a challenge to be honest with myself because my cunning mind can justify anything. For instance, on the work front, I am busy with a lot of different things, all of which are interesting and meaningful. But as I looked back at the things where I have made a difference, the times when I got the most satisfaction, the common thread has been developing leaders. The most important avenues for this going forward are my work with young people and entrepreneurs, inspiring a few people through my writing (this book for example) and speaking. Okay, then what about the other 10 things I am involved with? I found two or three of them to be important enablers of my commitment such as my work with Rockefeller Foundation or Hitachi, but most of the rest to be interesting distractions. The challenge now is to disentangle gracefully from some of these while doubling down on the primary commitments.

I think that it is in this bottom-up manner that you may find a way to articulate your purpose. Then you wear it for

a while and see if it fits, if it is authentic. When you find
that it is useful in prioritizing and saying *no* to things, you
know that you are on the right track. I am grateful to Russ
because he pushed me to become clearer about what matters
to me, what are important enablers and what is mere clutter
that is getting in the way. He helped me articulate what each
commitment looks like and also to see that I was over-indexing
on some commitments at the expense of others. Most of all,
he helped me see that only when you completely lose yourself
in service of something bigger than you, only when you stop
obsessing about yourself, can you be happy. This can be your
work, your faith or your marriage and family. The Hungarian
psychologist Mihaly Csikszentmihalyi said it really well, 'Only
when the self loses itself in a transcendent purpose—whether
to write great poetry, craft beautiful furniture, understand the
motions of galaxies, or help children be happier—does the
self becomes largely invulnerable to the fears and setbacks of
ordinary existence.'[80]

4. Accept that life is under no obligation to give you what you expect

This is what the late actor, Irrfan Khan, calmly said when
he was diagnosed with a terminal illness; his words stuck
with me. The fact is that life will not always or even largely
go as we expect. Life is what happens to us as we are busy
making other plans. It does not always feel fair. Irrfan did
not expect to die so young, but he dealt elegantly with his

---

[80]Mihaly Csikszentmihalyi, *Flow: The Psychology of Optimal Experience,* Harper
Perennial Modern Classics, 2008.

ailment; this inspired me.

As you reach midlife, even if things are going well, the thought occurs, 'Is this all there is? I had hoped for so much more.' It is quite common to have a sense that life is passing you by, that this is not how you imagined your life would turn out. It is easy to compare your situation with others who have it much better and start feeling bad for yourself. By our 40s, 50s and 60s, lightning strikes. There are catastrophic issues. Illnesses. Losses. Bad judgment and mistakes. It is not how you thought life would play out. *Why is this happening to me?*

'Why me?' is the wrong question. 'Why not you? What makes you so special that bad things happen only to other people?' asked my friend Anu, when I went moaning to her wanting sympathy when I hit a pothole. She should know having lived through the shock of losing both her husband and her son in short order. 'Ultimately, happiness lies in the enthusiastic, unambivalent acceptance of activities, situations and relationships that are not the best that might possibly be obtained,' wrote one psychologist. It does not matter what you expect from life but rather what life expects from you. In simpler language, happiness comes from wanting what you get rather than getting what you want. It comes from training yourself to see the positive in everything that happens and asking 'what am I supposed to learn from this?' I remember vividly when my friend Vijay was shot in a terrorist attack in Bengaluru. I went to visit him in the hospital. He had lost the use of his arm, which was devastating. But instead of being angry or depressed, he was cheerful and grateful to be alive. It made a huge impression on me and made my disappointments in life seem petty and churlish.

How do you deal with a huge setback, a devastating loss or a crisis? The best and most practical advice I got is called the Stockdale Paradox, after Vice Admiral James Stockdale, who was a prisoner of war during the Vietnam war and survived imprisonment and torture. It requires you to hold two opposing thoughts in your mind. The first is to confront and accept the brutal reality of your situation. Concurrently, you have to believe that life has handed you a tailor-made crucible for your growth, and to have hope and unwavering faith that you will prevail at the end, regardless of the difficulties and so work relentlessly and tenaciously till you do.

Cultivating such an acceptance is by no means easy; but like most things, it is a question of continuous practise. Every time negative thoughts and disappointments arise, instead of wallowing in them, I catch myself, think of Irrfan and say to myself, 'STOP! Life is under no obligation to give you what you expect,' and then I mentally count my blessings and say my thanks. This works slowly but surely just as a steady drip of water slowly wears down a rock.

5. Don't postpone living. Make a bucket list and get going

The COVID-19 pandemic has grimly reminded us that life is uncertain and it is wise not to postpone living. As Paulo Coelho said, 'We are such contradictions. We are in such a hurry to grow up, and then we long for our lost childhood. We think so much about the future that we neglect the present, and thus experience neither the present nor the future. We live as if we were never going to die, and die as if we had never lived.' Too many old people I know look back at their life with regret as they near their end but by then it is too late. I have seen too many lives extinguished prematurely particularly during the COVID-19 pandemic. Like many of you, I too have been postponing or deferring many things hoping to get to them someday. COVID-19 has reminded me to start living now.

One useful way to do this is through a thought exercise. If you had only this year to live, how would you live it? *The Bucket List* was a popular movie about two terminally ill old men who decide to embark on a set of experiences they'd always wanted but had postponed before finally kicking the bucket. So, making two bucket lists—one for this year and one for the future—is a useful exercise. Here are some things on my bucket list for this year:

  i.   Take a long vacation with my wife.
 ii.   Do another vipassana meditation retreat and get back to daily meditation.
iii.   Learn to make time for time. Prioritize my commitments and unwind several projects. Learn to say 'No' more often.
 iv.   Emerge from the long winter of COVID-19 by reconnecting in person with the people I like.

I have a small number of things in my longer-term, big bucket list:

  i.   Get back to running, overcoming the challenges of a damaged knee.
 ii.   Read all the books and listen to all the music that we own.
iii.   Ramp up our philanthropic giving to meaningful levels.

iv.   Visit every state in India.

v.   Radically declutter and reduce my possessions.

So, what's on your bucket list for this year? What's on your big bucket list?

KEY IDEAS

1. When you measure your life by someone else's definition of success, it tends to be subjective, fleeting and relative and therefore unsatisfying. Developing your authentic definition of how you will measure your life is difficult but critically important.

2. To control your happiness, control your mind. Both happiness and misery are synthesized by your mind and have fairly little to do with your reality. You have to learn to control your mind and not let your thoughts control you. Meditation practices like vipassana are very helpful for this.

3. Only when you stop living in a me-centric world, only when you completely lose yourself in the service of something bigger than you, only when you stop obsessing about yourself, can you be happy.

4. Ultimately, happiness lies in the enthusiastic, unambivalent acceptance of activities, situations and relationships that are not the best that might be obtained. Happiness comes from wanting what you get rather than getting what you want

5. Don't postpone living. Make your bucket list.

QUESTIONS FOR REFLECTION

1. Write down what success means to you. Are you actually living your life in pursuit of your definition of success or are you fooling yourself? Write down what actually drives your actions and behaviours—in reality this is how you are really defining success. Do you feel successful right now?

2. Write down your personal theory of happiness. What do you believe will make you happy? Are you generally happy and satisfied with your life?

3. Make a list of 10 people with whom you have ongoing interactions, such as family members, friends and colleagues. Ask each of them the two following questions:
   i.   What do they see in you?
   ii. How do they experience you?
   Encourage them to be very objective and to mention both the positive and negative qualities. Now, identify the patterns that evolve in this feedback. What do they tell you? Are there any changes you would like to make?

4. Do you have a monkey in your head? To what extent are you controlled by your mind and thoughts? Are you easily distracted, anxious or moody? When are you going to schedule a meditation retreat or begin a meditation practice? Have you considered downloading a meditation app?

5. Write down your commitments. What, at the end of the day, is most important to you? If you lived your life this way instead, would you have no regrets looking back? How are you actually spending your time and energy? What do you need to change?

6. Make your bucket list for this year and a big bucket list for life? List five things for each and schedule them even if they might be achieved only in the distant future.

7. Happiness is contagious. What can you do to make those around you happier?

Parting Thoughts

'We are not human beings having a spiritual experience;
we are spiritual beings having a human experience.'
—Pierre Teilhard de Chardin

∽

Quantum physics tells us that every particle is both a particle and a wave, and that particles are also transient, constantly popping in and out of existence. We human beings are the same; we are both human and divine, and just as transient. It is easy to lose sight of this and get caught up in the game of life, with its struggles and pleasures, with chasing success and happiness.

But from time to time, we get a glimmer of something much bigger, a sense that there is a bigger game and so these words from de Chardin resonate with us. Something deep within us knows that we are much more than our thoughts, emotions and circumstances, and that we are all part of something much larger. We come into the world with an innate awareness of our spiritual nature but through conditioning, we begin to identify with our transient thoughts, situations, our challenges and successes, and lose sight of how magnificent we are.

In school, we learnt about a magical biological process called metamorphosis—the process by which a caterpillar becomes a butterfly. A butterfly is not simply a bigger or more beautiful caterpillar. It is a fundamentally different form. There is no way you can see a caterpillar and imagine that it will eventually be a butterfly. It is sheer magic and a wonderful metaphor for our life.

The main point of our life is not to become a bigger or more successful caterpillar but to simply understand who we are, thereby releasing the spectacular butterfly within each of us. All the rest is but a means to this. As Helen Keller said, 'What I am looking for is not out there. It is in me.'

James G. March, professor of business, education and humanities at Stanford, and a person I admire deeply, summed it up superbly during an interview,

> In the end, we are very minor blips in a cosmic story. Aspirations for importance and significance are the illusions of the ignorant. All our hopes are minor except to us. But some things matter—mostly because we choose to make them matter. What might make a difference to us is if in our tiny roles, in our brief time, we inhabit life gently and add more beauty than ugliness.[81]

QUESTIONS FOR REFLECTION

1. What are the most useful or intriguing ideas from the book?
2. Which of these would you like to implement?

---

[81]Diane Coutou, 'Ideas As Art', *Harvard Business Review*, October 2006, https://hbr.org/2006/10/ideas-as-art. Accessed on 19 September 2021.

Acknowledgements

'If I have seen further,
it is by standing on the shoulders of giants.'
—Sir Isaac Newton

∽

Writing this book has been a monumental challenge and a nearly decade-long project. The reason for this has been the need to sort out my thinking and develop more clarity before writing about these issues. I don't have a big body of research and evidence to support my claims and assertions; I rely primarily on my lived experiences, my truth and the wisdom of people I respect. As a result, this book project has been an experiential process that has taken 10 years.

Another reason why this has been challenging is that at some level there is little that is original in what I have to say. The truth is that everything important about life and the pursuit of happiness has been said over 2,000 years ago by the Buddha, Hindu mystics, Greek philosophers and many others through the ages and that too in far more beautiful and compelling ways. All our hopes, struggles and dilemmas are much the same; only the context has changed. As a result, from time to time, I wondered whether there is any value in such a book. But then the consistently positive reception to small talks on these topics and the encouragement of friends and family convinced me that there is value to putting old ideas in a contemporary context—of pouring old wine into a new bottle using the filter of my own experiences. So that's what this is.

There is an extraordinarily large number of people who have contributed to this project, both knowingly and unknowingly. Many friends and colleagues of all ages (15–81) and from eight countries patiently reviewed various versions of the manuscript, helped me sharpen the ideas and encouraged me to keep going. I must acknowledge two people in particular. Yamini Chowdhury, the tenacious senior commissioning editor at Rupa, who has put up with innumerable delays without losing confidence. And my heroic wife, Sonali, who has had to endure my anxiety, doubts and distraction for all these years; this book has been a severe test of our friendship. I owe all of you a huge debt; this book is dedicated to you.

Note: *All proceeds from the sale of this book and from talks based on this book will be used to support various charities.*

Bibliography

Adam Davidson, *The Passion Economy: The New Rules for Thriving in the Twenty-First Century*, Knopf, 2020.

Adam Grant, *Think Again: The Power of Knowing What You Don't Know*, Penguin, 2021.

Adrian Wooldridge, 'Visors & Violence: We Are Returning to the Middle Ages', *The Economist*, 14 September 2020, https://www.economist.com/1843/2020/09/14/visors-and-violence-we-are-returning-to-the-middle-ages. Accessed on 10 September 2021.

Andrew J. Scott and Lynda Gratton, *The Hundred-Year Life—Living and Working in an Age of Longevity*, Bloomsbury Information, 2016.

Ben Ehrenreich, 'How Do You Know When Society Is About to Fall Apart?' *The New York Times*, 4 November 2020, https://www.nytimes.com/2020/11/04/magazine/societal-collapse.html. Accessed on 10 September 2021.

Bill Burnett and Dave Evans, 'Designing Your Life, Build the Perfect Career, Step by Step', https://designingyour.life/. Accessed on 10 September 2021.

Blair H. Sheppard, *Ten Years to Midnight: Four Urgent Global Crises and Their Strategic Solutions*, Berrett-Koehler, 2020.

Bob Buford, *Halftime: Moving from Success to Significance*, Zondervan, 2008.

Branco Milanovic, 'As the Pandemic Drives the Global Economy Apart, Societies May Break Apart, Too' *Foreign Affairs*, 9 June 2020, https://www.foreignaffairs.com/articles/2020-03-19/real-pandemic-danger-social-collapse. Accessed on 10 September 2021.

Carl Benedikt Frey, *Technology Trap: Capital, Labor, and Power in the Age of Automation*, Princeton University Press, 2020.

Carl Sagan, 'The Baloney Detection Kit', BrainPickings, https://www.brainpickings.org/2014/01/03/baloney-detection-kit-carl-sagan. Accessed on 10 September 2021.

Carol Dweck, *Mindset: The New Psychology of Success*, Random House, 2008.

Charles Handy, *21 Letters on Life and Its Challenges*, Random House, 2019.

Chris Argyris, 'Teaching Smart People How to Learn', *Harvard Business Review*, Issue: May–June 1991, https://hbr.org/1991/05/teaching-smart-people-how-to-learn. Accessed on 10 September 2021.

Clay M. Christensen, *How Will You Measure Your Life?* HarperCollins, 2012.

Daniel Gilbert, *Stumbling on Happiness*, Vintage Canada, 2009.

Daniel Kahneman, *Thinking, Fast and Slow*, Farrar, Straus and Giroux, 2011.

Daniel Susskind, *A World Without Work,* Metropolitan Books, 2020.

David Brooks, *The Second Mountain: The Quest for a Moral Life*, Random House, 2019.

David D. Corbett, *Portfolio Life: The New Path to Work, Purpose, and Passion After 50*, John Wiley & Sons, 2011.

David Epstein, *Range: Why Generalists Triumph in a Specialized World*, Penguin, 2021.

Deepak Jayaraman, 'Play to Potential', https://www.playtopotential.com. Accessed on 10 September 2021.

Douglas McGregor, *The Human Side of Enterprise*, McGraw Hill Professional, 2006.

Eckhart Tolle, *The Power of Now: A Guide to Spiritual Enlightenment*, New World Library, 1999.

Edmund S. Phelps, *Dynamism: The Values That Drive Innovation, Job Satisfaction, and Economic Growth*, Harvard University Press, 2020.

Eknath Easwaran, *Conquest of Mind: Take Charge of Your Thoughts and Reshape Your Life Through Meditation*, Nilgiri Press, 2010.

'Entrepreneurial Mindset', NFTE, https://www.nfte.com/entrepreneurial-mindset/. Accessed on 10 September 2021.

'Entrepreneurship Mindset Curriculum (EMC)', Udhyam Learning Foundation, https://docs.google.com/document/d/12pb6klBNyMsJs d8_0PeSNpJIuttmYUgZ_UuZQ6FLbE4/edit?usp=sharing. Accessed on 10 September 2021.

'Evidence Synthesis on the Impact of AI on work', Royal Society, https://royalsociety.org/-/media/policy/projects/ai-and-work/evidence-synthesis-the-impact-of-AI-on-work.PDF?la=en-GB&hash=A7BBF C34940375F2EE5548A1320F1F72. Accessed on 10 September 2021.

'Future of Work. The Salary Surge: Putting a Price on the Global Talent Crunch', Korn Ferry, https://www.kornferry.com/insights/this-week-in-leadership/the-salary-surge. Accessed on 10 September 2021.

Herminia Ibarra and Mark Lee Hunter, 'How Leaders Create and Use their Networks', *Harvard Business Review*, Issue: January 2007, https://hbr.org/2007/01/how-leaders-create-and-use-networks. Accessed on 10 September 2021.

Herminia Ibarra, *Working Identity: Nine Unconventional Strategies for Reinventing your Career,* Harvard Business Press, 2004.

Jacqueline T. Hill, 'How to Develop Self-Belief in 8 Steps', LifeHack, 14 December 2020, https://www.lifehack.org/871375/self-belief. Accessed on 10 September 2021.

James Currier, 'Your Life Is Driven by Network Effects', NFX, https://www.nfx.com/post/your-life-network-effects/

James Hollis, *Finding Meaning in the Second Half of Life*, Penguin, 2005.

John W. Gardner, *On Leadership*, Free Press, 1993.

Jonathan Haidt, *The Happiness Hypothesis: Finding Modern Truth in Ancient Wisdom*, Basic Books, 2006.

Jonathan Rauch, 'The Real Roots of Midlife Crisis', *The Atlantic*, December 2014, https://www.theatlantic.com/magazine/archive/2014/12/the-real-roots-of-midlife-crisis/382235/. Accessed on 10 September 2021.

Jonathan Rauch, *The Constitution of Knowledge: A Defense of Truth*, Brookings Institution Press, 2021.

Luke Kemp, 'Are We on the Road to Civilisation Collapse?' *BBC*, 19 February 2019, https://www.bbc.com/future/article/20190218-are-we-on-the-road-to-civilisation-collapse. Accessed on 10 September 2021.

M.K. Gandhi, *The Story of My Experiments with Truth*, Om Books International, 2009.

Marie Kondo, *The Life-Changing Magic of Tidying Up*, Ten Speed Press, 2014.

Marjorie Gerber, *Character: The History of a Cultural Obsession*, Farrar, Straus and Giroux, 2020.

Mark Muro, Robert Maxim and Jacob Whiton, 'Automation and Artificial Intelligence: How Machines Are Affecting People and Places', Brookings Institute, https://www.brookings.edu/research/automation-and-artificial-intelligence-how-machines-affect-people-and-places. Accessed on 10 September 2021.

Martin E.P. Seligman, *Learned Optimism—How to Change Your Mind and Your Life*, Vintage, 2011.

'Minimalism: A Documentary About the Important Things', Video Project, https://www.videoproject.com/Minimalism-Documentary.html. Accessed on 10 September 2021.

Nipun Mehta, 'Unlocking Multiple Forms of Wealth', Daily Good, 19 April 2016, http://www.dailygood.org/story/1260/unlocking-multiple-forms-of-wealth-nipun-mehta. Accessed on 10 September 2021.

'Our Programs', KidsWhoKode, https://www.kidswhokode.org/programs. Accessed on 10 September 2021.

Piero Ferrucci, *The Power of Kindness: The Unexpected Benefits of Leading a Compassionate Life*, Penguin, 2016.

Prof. Teresa Amabile, 'How Retirement Changes Your Identity', *Harvard Business Review*, 15 January 2019, https://hbr.org/podcast/2019/01/how-retirement-changes-your-identity. Accessed on 10 September 2021.

Ravi Venkatesan, *Conquering the Chaos: Win in India, Win Everywhere*, Harvard Business School Press, 2013.

Sara Lawrence-Lightfoot, *The Third Chapter: Passion, Risk, and Adventure in the 25 Years After 50*, Sarah Crichton Books, 2009.

Seph Fontane Pennock, 'The Hedonic Treadmill—Are We Forever Chasing Rainbows?' Positive Psychology, 25 November 2021, https://positivepsychology.com/hedonic-treadmill/. Accessed on 5 December 2021.

Shamika Ravi, 'View: Here's what we know for sure about jobs in India', *The Economic Times*, 18 April 2019, https://economictimes.indiatimes.com/news/economy/policy/heres-what-we-know-for-sure-about-jobs-in-india/articleshow/68916626.cms. Accessed on 10 September 2021.

Snigdha Poonam, *Dreamers: How Young Indians Are Changing the World*, Harvard University Press, 2018.

Srikant Rao, 'Rewiring Your Mind for Greater Happiness and Success', YouTube, https://www.youtube.com/watch?v=vBlWbV64N4I. Accessed on 10 September 2021.

Stephen Covey, *The 7 Habits of Highly Effective People*, Simon & Schuster, 2013.

'Student Leader-Rehan', Global Learning Lab, Vimeo, https://vimeo.com/356868885. Accessed on 10 September 2021.

Susan Lund, Anu Madgavkar, James Manyika, Sven Smit, Kweilin Ellingrud and Olivia Robinson, 'The Future of Work after COVID-19', McKinsey Global Institute, 18 February 2021, https://www.mckinsey.com/featured-insights/future-of-work/the-future-of-work-after-covid-19. Accessed on 10 September 2021.

'The Act of Reaching Out', SoundCloud, https://soundcloud.com/radionazariya107-8fm/the-act-of-reaching-out. Accessed on 10 September 2021.

Timothy Ferriss, *The 4-Hour Workweek*, Harmony, 2009.

Viktor E. Frankl, *Man's Search for Meaning*, Random House, 2008.

Warren Berger, 'Carl Sagan's Logical Fallacies: How to Teach Yourself to Be a Better Critical Thinker', Quartz, https://qz.com/915723/want-to-be-a-better-critical-thinker-heres-how-to-spot-false-narratives-and-weaponized-lies/. Accessed on 10 September 2021.

'"You've Got to Find What You Love," Jobs Says', Stanford News, 14 June 2005, https://news.stanford.edu/2005/06/14/jobs-061505/. Accessed on 10 September 2021.

Yuval Noah Harari, *Sapiens: A Brief History of Humankind*, HarperCollins, 2015.

Index